ASIAN POLITICAL, ECONOMIC AND SECURITY ISSUES

MALAYSIA

CONDITIONS, ISSUES AND U.S. RELATIONS

ASIAN POLITICAL, ECONOMIC AND SECURITY ISSUES

Additional books in this series can be found on Nova's website under the Series tab.

Additional e-books in this series can be found on Nova's website under the e-book tab.

ASIAN POLITICAL, ECONOMIC AND SECURITY ISSUES

MALAYSIA

CONDITIONS, ISSUES AND U.S. RELATIONS

PAULINA COLLINS
EDITOR

nova publishers
New York

For permission to use material from this book please contact us:
Telephone 631-231-7269; Fax 631-231-8175
Web Site: http://www.novapublishers.com

Library of Congress Cataloging-in-Publication Data

ISBN: 978-1-63321-227-5

Published by Nova Science Publishers, Inc. † New York

CONTENTS

PREFACE

Malaysia, a majority Muslim nation in Southeast Asia, has long been a partner in U.S. security and economic initiatives in the region, although political sensitivities in Malaysia have constrained both sides from forging deeper ties or even acknowledging how close the relationship is. Bilateral relations have improved over the past decade, especially under Prime Minister Najib Razak, who has made relations with the United States a priority. The Obama Administration has emphasized deeper engagement with Malaysia and other "emerging partners" in Southeast Asia as part of the strategic "rebalancing" of U.S. resources and attention to the Asia-Pacific region. Congress has expressed interest in a variety of issues in U.S.-Malaysia relations over the years, especially regarding trade, security cooperation, human rights, and Malaysia's diplomacy. This book analyzes U.S.-Malaysia relations and the economy, domestic politics, and diplomacy of Malaysia. The book also provides background information on current events and policy debates related to Malaysia.

Chapter 1 – Malaysia, a majority Muslim nation in Southeast Asia, has long been a partner in U.S. security and economic initiatives in the region, although political sensitivities in Malaysia have constrained both sides from forging deeper ties or even acknowledging how close the relationship is. Bilateral relations have improved over the past decade, especially under Prime Minister Najib Razak, who has made relations with the United States a priority. The Obama Administration has emphasized deeper engagement with Malaysia and other "emerging partners" in Southeast Asia as part of the strategic "rebalancing" of U.S. resources and attention to the Asia-Pacific region. Congress has expressed interest in a variety of issues in U.S.-Malaysia relations over the years, especially regarding trade, security cooperation, human rights, and Malaysia's diplomacy. The two nations are major trade and investment partners. In 2013, Malaysia was the 25th largest market for U.S. exports and the 18th largest supplier of U.S. imports. The United States was Malaysia's 4th largest export market (after Singapore, China, and Japan) and the 4th largest supplier of imports (after China, Singapore, and Japan). Both countries are parties to the Trans-Pacific Partnership (TPP) negotiations, which aim to create a high-standards free trade agreement among 12 countries comprising nearly 40% of the global economy. The United States' main trade-related concerns are Malaysia's government procurement policies, protection of intellectual property rights, and market access for key goods and services. Despite a diverse ethnic and religious mix, Malaysia has enjoyed considerable political stability since it gained independence in 1957. Political coalitions led by the United Malays National Organization (UMNO), the country's dominant political party, have ruled Malaysia without interruption since independence. UMNO is a staunch proponent of the preeminent position of ethnic Malays and other indigenous groups, collectively known as *bumiputra*. The United States occasionally has criticized the Malaysian government for its weak human rights protections, constraints on press freedom, and prosecution of opposition political leaders like Anwar Ibrahim. Malaysia achieved high rates of GDP growth through the 1970s and into the 1990s, as did other East Asian economies. It is now considered a middle-income country, relatively prosperous compared to most other Southeast Asian countries, and has retained its Muslim identity through periods of rapid modernization. As in politics, Malaysia's economy is divided along regional and ethnic lines; a wide ranging economic program known as the New Economic Policy attempts to address socio-economic disparities by privileging ethnic Malays and other indigenous groups in government contracts, education, and government hiring. Malaysia has been a constructive diplomatic actor on numerous regional and global issues. Efforts to promote moderate Islam and marginalize religious extremism have been a major part of Malaysian diplomacy, including acting as a mediator in conflicts between Muslim separatist groups and the central government in both Thailand and the Philippines. Kuala Lumpur maintains good relations with its neighbors and has promoted cooperation among the 10 countries in the Association of Southeast Asian Nations (ASEAN). Malaysia is one of several Southeast Asian countries with maritime and territorial claims in the South China Sea, although it has assumed a low profile in those disputes. U.S.-Malaysia security cooperation includes counter-terrorism activities, numerous military exercises, ship visits, and military education exchanges.

Chapter 2 – Malaysia is a federal constitutional monarchy. It has a parliamentary system of government selected through periodic, multi-party elections and headed by a prime minister. The king is the head of state and serves a largely ceremonial role; the kingship rotates among the nine sultans every five years. The United Malays National Organization (UMNO), together with a coalition of political parties known as the National Front (BN), has held power since independence in 1957. On May 5, in general elections, the BN was re-elected although it lost the popular vote to the opposition coalition. The opposition and civil society organizations alleged electoral irregularities. Civilian authorities failed at times to maintain effective control over security forces. Security forces committed human rights abuses. The most significant human rights problems included obstacles preventing opposition parties from competing on equal terms with the ruling coalition; restrictions on freedoms of speech, assembly, association, and religion; and restrictions on freedom of the press, including media bias, book banning, censorship, and the denial of printing permits. Other human rights problems included deaths during police apprehension and while in police custody; the persistence of laws that allow detention without trial; caning as a form of punishment imposed by criminal and sharia courts; bans on religious groups; restrictions on proselytizing and on the freedom to change one's religion; official corruption; violence and discrimination against women; discrimination against lesbian, gay, bisexual, and transgender (LGBT) persons; and restrictions on the rights of migrants, including migrant workers, refugees, and victims of human trafficking. Longstanding government policies gave preferences to ethnic Malays in many areas. The government restricted union and collective- bargaining activity, and government policies created vulnerabilities and worsened child labor and forced labor problems, especially for migrant workers. The government prosecuted some officials engaged in corruption and human rights abuses, although some degree of impunity continued.

Chapter 3 – The constitution protects religious freedom with some exceptions. Portions of the constitution, as well as other laws and policies, place some restrictions on religious freedom and in practice the government generally enforced those restrictions. The trend in the government's respect for religious freedom did not change significantly during the year. The constitution gives federal and state governments the power to "control or restrict the propagation of any religious doctrine or belief among persons professing the religion of Islam." The government maintains a dual legal system, under which Sharia courts rule on religious, family, and some criminal issues involving Muslims and secular courts rule on other issues pertaining to both Muslims and the broader population. Government policies promote Sunni Islam above other religions. Other teachings and forms of Islam are illegal, and the government maintains an official but secret list of banned sects of Islam. The constitution defines ethnic Malays as Muslim from birth. Muslims may not legally convert to another religion except in extremely rare circumstances, although members of other religions may convert to Islam. Minority religious groups remained generally free to practice their beliefs. There were reports of societal abuse and discrimination based on religious affiliation, belief, or practice, including reports of child marriages as an approved practice of Islam. Civil society organizations continued to criticize this practice. Embassy representatives maintained an active dialogue with the government and with leaders and representatives of various religious groups, including those not officially recognized by the government. The ambassador visited and met with religious leaders across the country to emphasize the importance of religious freedom and tolerance among religions.

Chapter 4 – The Government of Malaysia in general strongly encourages foreign direct investment (FDI), although it maintains restrictions or limits on investment in some sectors. It actively reaches out to targeted industries and negotiates incentive packages to attract FDI. Malaysia provides a number of incentives, particularly in export-oriented high-tech industries and "back office" service operations. A wide range of U.S. companies have extensive operations in Malaysia. Prime Minister Najib Razak (Najib) has made generating new domestic and foreign investment a centerpiece of his economic reform program introduced in March 2010 as the New Economic Model (NEM). Although FDI inflow continues to recover from the effects of the 2008-2009 global financial crises, Malaysia's performance in attracting FDI relative to both earlier decades and the rest of the Association of Southeast Asian Nations (ASEAN) has slowed. According to a recent Organization for Economic Cooperation and Development (OECD) Investment Policy Review of Malaysia, FDI to Malaysia began to decline in 1992, and private investment overall started to slide in 1997 following the Asian financial crises. Today, FDI levels are at record high levels in absolute terms, but at an all-time low as a percentage of GDP. Moreover, Malaysia's percentage of overall investment in the ASEAN member states is now lower than its share of the group's GDP. The National Economic Advisory Council (NEAC), a blue ribbon panel of experts on Malaysia's economy, in 2010 issued two reports identifying shortcomings in Malaysia's investment climate and proposing policies necessary to improve Malaysia's competitiveness as a foreign investment destination and meet the country's goal of becoming a high-income economy by 2020. Since then, the Najib administration has progressively introduced a series of initiatives to implement the NEM. One initiative, the Economic Transformation Program (ETP), is focused on investment in 12 key economic areas to accelerate economic growth; and a set of policy measures to improve competitiveness. Another initiative, the Government Transformation Program (GTP) addresses governance and quality of life issues, and aims to reduce corruption and crime, to improve education, urban public transport and rural basic infrastructure, and to reduce the number of low-income households. The Tenth Malaysia Plan (10MP) underpins these programs and guides public sector capital expenditures. Inflows of actual FDI to Malaysia in 2011 increased to US$10.9 billion, up 12.3% from $9.7 billion in 2010 according to the UN Conference on Trade and Development (UNCTAD). According to the Malaysian Investment Development Authority (MIDA), the total value of foreign manufacturing projects approved in 2011 was US$10.77 billion. The 2011 manufacturing FDI approvals were 13.36% higher than US$9.5 billion in 2010. The U.S., Japan, and Hong Kong are the top three countries investing in Malaysia. Up to September 2012, MIDA had approved foreign manufacturing projects worth US$5.25 billion, with Saudi Arabia the largest source of new approved investments.

In: Malaysia
Editor: Paulina Collins
ISBN: 978-1-63321-227-5

Chapter 1

MALAYSIA: BACKGROUND AND U.S. RELATIONS*

Ian E. Rinehart

SUMMARY

Malaysia, a majority Muslim nation in Southeast Asia, has long been a partner in U.S. security and economic initiatives in the region, although political sensitivities in Malaysia have constrained both sides from forging deeper ties or even acknowledging how close the relationship is. Bilateral relations have improved over the past decade, especially under Prime Minister Najib Razak, who has made relations with the United States a priority. The Obama Administration has emphasized deeper engagement with Malaysia and other "emerging partners" in Southeast Asia as part of the strategic "rebalancing" of U.S. resources and attention to the Asia-Pacific region. Congress has expressed interest in a variety of issues in U.S.-Malaysia relations over the years, especially regarding trade, security cooperation, human rights, and Malaysia's diplomacy.

The two nations are major trade and investment partners. In 2013, Malaysia was the 25th largest market for U.S. exports and the 18th largest supplier of U.S. imports. The United States was Malaysia's 4th largest export

* This is an edited, reformatted and augmented version of a Congressional Research Service publication R43505, prepared for Members and Committees of Congress dated April 21, 2014.

market (after Singapore, China, and Japan) and the 4th largest supplier of imports (after China, Singapore, and Japan). Both countries are parties to the Trans-Pacific Partnership (TPP) negotiations, which aim to create a high-standards free trade agreement among 12 countries comprising nearly 40% of the global economy. The United States' main trade-related concerns are Malaysia's government procurement policies, protection of intellectual property rights, and market access for key goods and services.

Despite a diverse ethnic and religious mix, Malaysia has enjoyed considerable political stability since it gained independence in 1957. Political coalitions led by the United Malays National Organization (UMNO), the country's dominant political party, have ruled Malaysia without interruption since independence. UMNO is a staunch proponent of the preeminent position of ethnic Malays and other indigenous groups, collectively known as *bumiputra*. The United States occasionally has criticized the Malaysian government for its weak human rights protections, constraints on press freedom, and prosecution of opposition political leaders like Anwar Ibrahim.

Malaysia achieved high rates of GDP growth through the 1970s and into the 1990s, as did other East Asian economies. It is now considered a middle-income country, relatively prosperous compared to most other Southeast Asian countries, and has retained its Muslim identity through periods of rapid modernization. As in politics, Malaysia's economy is divided along regional and ethnic lines; a wide ranging economic program known as the New Economic Policy attempts to address socio-economic disparities by privileging ethnic Malays and other indigenous groups in government contracts, education, and government hiring.

Malaysia has been a constructive diplomatic actor on numerous regional and global issues. Efforts to promote moderate Islam and marginalize religious extremism have been a major part of Malaysian diplomacy, including acting as a mediator in conflicts between Muslim separatist groups and the central government in both Thailand and the Philippines. Kuala Lumpur maintains good relations with its neighbors and has promoted cooperation among the 10 countries in the Association of Southeast Asian Nations (ASEAN). Malaysia is one of several Southeast Asian countries with maritime and territorial claims in the South China Sea, although it has assumed a low profile in those disputes. U.S.-Malaysia security cooperation includes counter-terrorism activities, numerous military exercises, ship visits, and military education exchanges.

Introduction

This report analyzes U.S.-Malaysia relations and the economy, domestic politics, and diplomacy of Malaysia. Congress has expressed interest in a variety of issues in U.S.-Malaysia relations, especially regarding trade, security cooperation, and human rights. The report provides background information on current events and policy debates related to Malaysia.[1]

Overview

The relationship between the United States and Malaysia is a complex one. Bilateral ties are considerably closer than often is acknowledged, but lingering mistrust and political sensitivities in Malaysia constrain the establishment of a deeper strategic relationship. Malaysia, a majority Muslim nation of 30 million people, is a partner in numerous U.S. security and economic initiatives in Southeast Asia. It is a major U.S. trading partner and a site of substantial U.S. investment. Malaysia, for many years one of the leading voices behind building "Asia-only" regional institutions, is now seen as an advocate of a strong U.S. presence in the Asia-Pacific region. Some experts believe that Malaysian concerns about China's assertiveness in the South China Sea have been the main driver behind closer U.S.-Malaysia strategic ties.[2] Yet, some issues have proven contentious over recent years—particularly U.S. counter-terrorism strategy and policy in the Middle East—and many observers still perceive a ceiling on the degree to which the two countries can deepen their relationship.

The Obama Administration's strategic "rebalancing" of foreign policy priorities to Asia has placed substantially increased attention on the nations of Southeast Asia, including Malaysia. Although the rebalancing has not featured high-profile bilateral initiatives with Malaysia, most observers say U.S.-Malaysia relations have warmed considerably in recent years. Malaysia is one of 12 nations negotiating the Trans Pacific Partnership (TPP), a potential trade agreement that is the United States' highest-priority economic initiative in Asia. The United States and Malaysia also conduct numerous military exchanges, training exercises, and port visits and cooperate in counter-terrorism and maritime domain awareness.

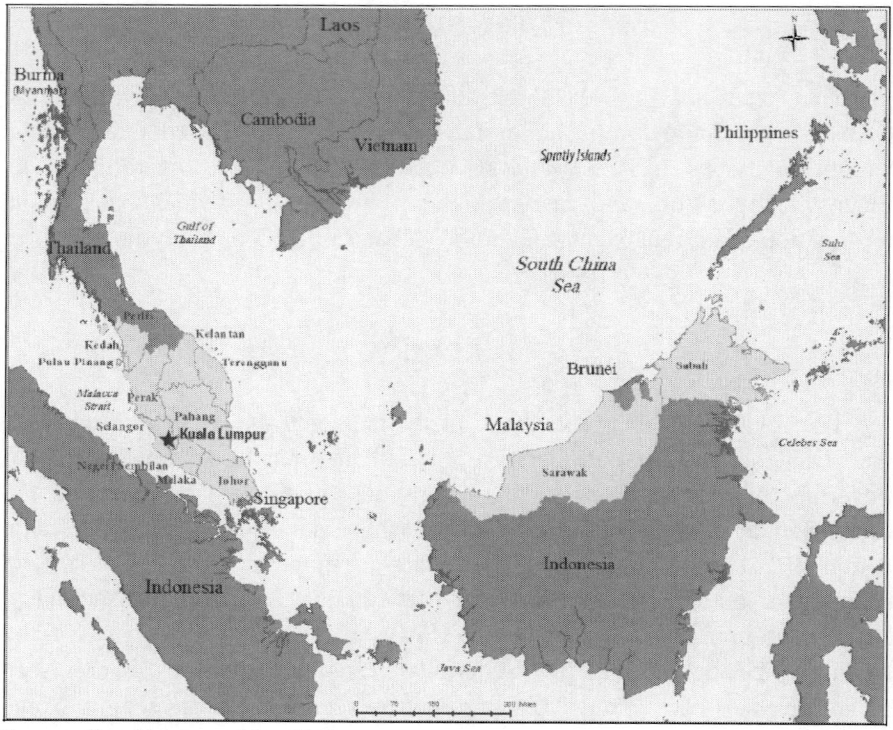

Source: Graphic created by CRS.

Figure 1. Malaysia and Surrounding Areas.

Malaysia harbors a strong self-image as a moderate leader within the Islamic world, and this role sometimes complicates its relationship with the United States. Malaysia has criticized the U.S. counter-terrorism strategy and its support for Israel, maintaining that these policies created a perception that the United States was "anti-Islam," and that U.S. rhetoric generated broader support for Islamic militancy. However, Malaysian statements along these lines have moderated in recent years, especially under the current Prime Minister, Najib Razak.

Modern Malaysian History

For most of its early history, the territory that comprises the modern state of Malaysia was a collection of small, separate kingdoms or sultanates. After Islam was introduced to Southeast Asia by Muslim traders, most of the indigenous population adopted the religion. In the late 18th through mid-19th centuries, during the height of European imperialism, various principalities on the Malaysian Peninsula and northern Borneo fell under the British sphere of influence. Britain administered these resource-rich states through local leaders and eventually knit together these territories into the Federated Malay States in 1895. Japan briefly ousted the European powers from Southeast Asia during World War II, but Britain restored its governance of the Malaysian territories after 1945, inaugurating the Federation of Malaya in 1948.

While indigenous political groups, including the United Malays National Organization (UMNO), agitated for independence during the postwar period, the Malayan Communist Party waged a prolonged guerrilla campaign against British rule. The British and their anti-Communist allies in Malaysia defeated the Communist campaign, sometimes employing brutal tactics; this period is known as "the Emergency." Peninsular Malaya gained its independence as a constitutional monarchy in 1957, and the colonies of Singapore, Sabah, and Sarawak were relinquished by Britain in 1963 into the new Federation of Malaysia. Indonesian ruler Sukarno opposed this union and instigated low-level military conflict (known as *konfrontasi*) with newly enlarged Malaysia until 1965. Singapore was forced out of the federation and became independent in 1965 amid a series of political disagreements between Malaysian and Singaporean leaders.

Race riots between Malays and Chinese that erupted in May 1969 in Kuala Lumpur shook the social foundations of Malaysia and catalyzed reform of the political system. A major consequence of the race riots was the New Economic Policy (NEP), which sought to remedy socioeconomic disparities by favoring *bumiputra*—ethnic Malays and other indigenous groups—over the economically dominant Chinese minority. The Malaysian government promoted agricultural improvements, natural resource exploitation, and export-oriented industrialization (reserving opportunities for *bumiputra*) that led to consistent economic growth through the 1970s and 1980s.

In the political sphere, the UMNO-led coalition of ethnically based parties has maintained its preeminence since independence and delivered a measure of stability to Malaysia despite internal diversity and a volatile external security environment. A central figure in recent Malaysian history is Mahathir Mohamad, who was Prime Minister from 1981 until 2003 and remains politically active. Mahathir helped to shape a more secular Malaysia by limiting the political strength of religious leaders and curtailing the privileges of Malaysia's royalty. He also aggressively sought to rein in critical voices in the political arena, the media, and civil society. Many aspects of Malaysia's current political landscape have evolved from the Mahathir era, as both prime ministers who followed him, as well as opposition leader Anwar Ibrahim, were at one time his protégés within UMNO.

Challenges for Malaysia

Malaysia faces numerous internal and external challenges as it seeks to attain its goal of becoming a prosperous, developed country that is influential in Southeast Asia and around the world. Chief among Malaysia's domestic challenges are ethnic and religious sensitivities and tensions, a volatile political climate with an increasingly active political opposition, and fragile protections for human rights. Compared to most of its Southeast Asian neighbors, Malaysia has a relatively high average income, but its economy is still undergoing the transition to high technology, high value-added industries. Many economic reform proposals confront opposition from rural, Malay-centric interest groups. As one of the leading countries in ASEAN (the Association of Southeast Asian Nations), Malaysia faces the diplomatic challenges of promoting regional trade integration, maintaining security and stability, and creating an attractive climate for outside investment. The rise of China brings many opportunities to East Asian countries, as well as concern about Beijing's increasing assertiveness in regional affairs.

BASIC DATA

Population: 30,040,000 (April 2014 est.)

Area: 126,895 sq. mi. (slightly larger than New Mexico)

Gross domestic product (GDP): $326.3 billion (2013)

Per capita GDP: $10,895

Ethnicities: Malay/*bumiputra* 67%, Chinese 25%, Indian 7%, others 1%

Religions: Islam 61%, Buddhism 20%, Christianity 9%, Hinduism 6%, others 2%

Life expectancy at birth: male 72 years, female 77 years

Government type: Federal Constitutional Monarchy (Parliamentary Democracy)

Prime Minister: Mohamed NAJIB bin Abdul Najib Razak (inaugurated April 3, 2009)

Sources: Population, ethnicity, religion, and life expectancy data from Malaysian Department of Statistics. GDP data from Malaysia's Economic Planning Unit.

U.S.-MALAYSIA POLITICAL RELATIONS

Bilateral ties between the United States and Malaysia long have been both highly cooperative and publicly contentious. Malaysia is a strong partner in many U.S. security and economic initiatives, but domestic Malaysian sensitivities, particularly regarding the nation's identity in the Muslim world, have consistently constrained Malaysian leaders from undertaking high-profile partnerships with the United States.

The Obama Administration's strategic "rebalancing" to the Asia-Pacific region has placed a high priority on deepening relations with Southeast Asian countries, and Malaysian Prime Minister Najib Razak has spoken frequently about building stronger relations with the United States. With its participation in the TPP negotiations, Malaysia is part of the Administration's signature economic initiative in the region. President Obama's April 2014 visit to Malaysia makes him the first U.S. President to visit the country since 1966. (Obama's scheduled visit in October 2013 was cancelled due to the partial U.S. government shutdown.)

The Najib government has taken visible steps to support U.S. initiatives. In April 2010, Malaysia enacted legislation to strengthen its restrictions on the shipment of nuclear materials, on the eve of the Nuclear Security Summit hosted by President Obama. In 2010, it sent 40 military medical personnel to Bamiyan province in Afghanistan, and it subsequently has rotated four deployments to support Afghan reconstruction—a notably public move in a Muslim-majority nation where U.S. actions in Iraq had led to large protests at the U.S. Embassy in Kuala Lumpur.

The high visibility of these initiatives marks a change for the bilateral relationship. U.S. relations with Malaysia were particularly fraught under long-time Prime Minister Mahathir, who was a vocal advocate of "Asia-only" regional organizations. Malaysians were particularly upset both by U.S. criticism of Malaysia's economic policy during the Asian Financial Crisis in 1998, when Malaysia instituted strong controls on capital flows in order to protect its currency; and by high-level U.S. criticism of Malaysia's judiciary after Anwar Ibrahim, then Malaysia's Deputy Prime Minister, was arrested and subsequently convicted of sodomy, which is a crime under Malaysian law. (See "Domestic Politics", below.) Following Mahathir's retirement as Prime Minister in 2003 (he remains a politically active Member of Parliament), some of the barriers to warmer bilateral ties eased, although Malaysia continues to strongly oppose U.S. support for Israel. Washington and Kuala Lumpur agreed to discuss a Free Trade Agreement in 2005, and although those negotiations did not ultimately conclude in an agreement, Malaysia is an active participant in the TPP negotiations.

The United States periodically has raised concerns about human rights and democracy issues in Malaysia. In March 2014, after Malaysia's highest appeals court overturned the acquittal of Anwar Ibrahim, now a prominent opposition leader, on a separate sodomy charge—a decision that many observers deemed politically motivated and that potentially barred Anwar from seeking a state governership—the U.S. State Department said, "The decision to prosecute Mr. Anwar and his trial have raised a number of concerns regarding the rule of law and the independence of the courts."[3]

The official U.S. reaction to Malaysia's most recent nationwide parliamentary elections in May 2013, in which opposition parties alleged that widespread electoral fraud contributed to the ruling coalition's victory, was muted. A State Department spokesman said, "We were pleased to see Malaysians across the political spectrum engaged in the electoral process in large numbers with unprecedented enthusiasm." He also noted, however, "We are aware of concerns about voting irregularities and note that the opposition parties faced significant restrictions on access to the media. Addressing these issues is important to strengthen confidence in the electoral process."[4]

MALAYSIA'S ECONOMY

Prior to the 2008 global financial crisis, Malaysia had been one of the fastest growing economies in the world over the past 25 years (see **Table 1**). Malaysia was able to recover from the global recession and an economic downturn in 2009 comparatively quickly, and its economic performance in early 2014 was close to its pre-crisis level. At the same time, however, Prime Minister Najib remained under some domestic pressure to find ways of achieving the nation's self-proclaimed goal of becoming a developed nation by 2020, while addressing the country's regional and income disparities.

Malaysia's economy is regionally and sectorally diversified. The State of Selangor, which surrounds the capital of Kuala Lumpur, is the largest contributor to the nation's GDP, followed by Kuala Lumpur. The State of Johor, located next to Singapore, and the State of Sarawak, on the island of Borneo, also are significant contributors to the GDP. These four regions are Malaysia's most prosperous areas and form the core for the nation's manufacturing and services sectors. By contrast, the states of Kedah, Kelantan, Perak, and Perlis, along the border with Thailand, as well as the State of Sabah on the northern tip of the island of Borneo, are relatively poorer regions of Malaysia with less manufacturing and services activity.

Malaysia also is economically divided along urban/rural lines and between its ethnicities. Malaysia's urban centers, such as Kuala Lumpur, are relatively prosperous and support a growing middle class, while its rural areas are comparatively underdeveloped. Malaysia's major ethnic groups face differing economic conditions. The Chinese-Malaysians are generally prosperous and play an important role in the nation's commercial and trade sectors. The Indian-Malaysians are split into a comparatively wealthy few and a comparatively poor many. Though they constitute a majority of the population, Malays and other indigenous people (i.e., *bumiputra*), traditionally have been considered economically disadvantaged, leading to the 1971 introduction of the New Economic Policy (NEP) mentioned above.

Table 1. Selected Indicators for Malaysia's Economy

	2007	2008	2009	2010	2011	2012	2013
Real GDP Growth	6.3%	4.8%	-1.5%	7.2%	5.1%	5.6%	5.0-6.0%
Nominal GDP (billions of U.S dollars)	193.6	231.0	202.3	246.8	287.9	303.5	326.3
Per Capita Income (U.S. dollars)	7,218	8,460	7,278	8,729	10,012	10,381	10,687
Inflation Rate—CPI	6.4%	6.1%	0.6%	1.7%	3.2%	1.7%	2.0-3.0%
Unemployment Rate	3.3%	3.3%	3.7%	3.4%	N.A.	N.A.	3.1%
Exchange Rate (Ringgits/$)	3.44	3.33	3.52	3.22	3.06	3.09	3.09

Sources: 2007-2012 data from the World Bank; 2013 data from Malaysia's Economic Planning Unit.

Notes: GDP—gross domestic product; CPI—consumer price index; N.A.—not available.

Roughly half of Malaysia's GDP comes from the services sector. Manufacturing provides an additional 26% of GDP and mining contributes 13%. Agriculture supplies 11% of GDP. Trade-related services (such as finance, insurance, and business services) and tourism-related services dominate the services sector. Malaysia mainly manufactures consumer electronics, much of it parts and components for export and use in regional manufacturing supply chains. Malaysia exports three major crops: cocoa, palm oil, and rubber.

TRADE RELATIONS WITH THE UNITED STATES

Malaysia is a significant trading partner for the United States, but the United States is an even more important trading partner for Malaysia. In 2013, Malaysia was the 25th largest market for U.S. exports and the 18th largest supplier of U.S. imports. By contrast, the United States was Malaysia's 4th largest export market (after Singapore, China, and Japan) and the 4th largest supplier of imports (after China, Singapore, and Japan).

The two nations report significantly different amounts for their bilateral trade, with the United States listing higher values for imports from Malaysia and lower values for exports to Malaysia over the last five years (see **Table 2**).[5] As a result, the United States reports a higher bilateral trade deficit with Malaysia, while Malaysia reports a lower bilateral trade surplus.

Table 2. Official Merchandise Trade Figures:Malaysia and United States (U.S. dollars in billions)

	Malaysia Trade Data		U.S. Trade Data	
Year	Exports to United States	Imports from United States	Imports from Malaysia	Exports to Malaysia
2013	N.A.	N.A.	$27.3	$13.0
2012	$19.7	$15.9	$26.7	$12.9
2011	$18.9	$18.1	$26.5	$14.2
2010	$19.0	$17.5	$26.6	$14.0
2009	$17.3	$13.9	$23.9	$10.4
2008	$24.9	$17.0	$31.6	$13.0

Source: International Monetary Fund, *Direction of Trade Statistics*; U.S. International Trade Commission.

In merchandise trade, electrical machinery and equipment dominate trade flows in both directions, reflecting Malaysia's role as a major source for consumer electronics. According to official 2013 U.S. trade data, $5.4 billion in electrical machinery and equipment (as listed under harmonized tariff schedule (HS) 85) was exported to Malaysia and $14.8 billion was imported from Malaysia, representing 42% of total exports and 54% of total imports. Other major exports to Malaysia were (in order) aircraft and aircraft parts (HS 88)—$1.6 billion; and machinery and mechanical equipment (HS 84)—$1.4 billion. Other major imports from Malaysia were (in order) machinery and mechanical appliances (HS 84) —$4.0 billion; optical, photographic, cinematographic, medical or surgical instruments and apparatus (HS 90)—$1. 6 billion; and rubber and rubber articles (HS 40)—$1.4 billion.

According to the U.S. Bureau of Economic Analysis (BEA), U.S. services exports to Malaysia in 2012 totaled $2.45 billion, and services imports from Malaysia totaled $1.36 billion. About one-third of U.S. services exports to Malaysia and over half of the services imports from Malaysia were business, professional, or technical services.

Over 600 U.S. companies operate in Malaysia, many in the electronics and information technology industries. Total U.S. foreign direct investment (FDI) in Malaysia as of the end of 2012 was $12.39 billion. Roughly half of this was in manufacturing (largely electronics), and about a quarter was in mining. By contrast, Malaysia has very little FDI in the United States. According to BEA, the total value of Malaysia's FDI in the United States as of 2012 was $662 million.

Trans-Pacific Partnership Negotiations

Both Malaysia and the United States are parties to the ongoing negotiations to create a new trade agreement known as the Trans-Pacific Partnership (TPP).[6] The United States entered into negotiations with the four members (P4)—Brunei, Chile, New Zealand, and Singapore—of the Trans-Pacific Strategic Economic Partnership in 2008. Malaysia was accepted as the ninth negotiating party in October 2010.[7] The Obama Administration has made the successful conclusion of the TPP talks a major priority for its international trade policy.[8]

Prior to joining the TPP talks, Malaysia had been negotiating a bilateral trade agreement with the United States since March 2006.[9] In October 2010, the U.S. Trade Representative officially notified Congress that the bilateral trade talks would be folded into the TPP negotiations. Talks on the bilateral trade agreement reportedly had stalled on several issues, including

- Malaysia's government procurement policies, which give preferential treatment for certain types of Malaysian-owned companies;
- provisions for intellectual property rights (IPR) protection; and
- market access for key commodities and services.

These same issues reportedly pose problems in the TPP negotiations. The language in a proposed chapter on state-owned enterprises has supposedly been an area where the United States and Malaysia have significant differences of opinion.[10] One issue on which Malaysian TPP negotiators reportedly have found common ground with at least some Americans engaged in TPP-related advocacy is a proposed exclusion of tobacco. A letter signed by 45 U.S. state attorneys general in January 2014 called on the U.S. Trade Representative (USTR) to support the Malaysian proposal to "carve out" tobacco from all provisions of the TPP.[11] They asserted that this measure would "preserve the ability of state and local governments to regulate tobacco products to protect the public health." Meanwhile, the USTR has advanced an alternative proposal that contains general exceptions necessary to protect life and health—and applies those to tobacco—but allows the invocation of dispute settlement over tobacco control regulations.

Prime Minister Najib repeatedly has expressed his support for the TPP but faces strong opposition to the trade agreement at home. Malaysia's farmers want greater access to the U.S. market, but are concerned about increased competition from U.S. agricultural exporters. Some Malaysian manufacturing sectors are apprehensive about increased competition from major U.S. corporations. Malaysia's health care providers and the population in general are worried about access to affordable pharmaceuticals if IPR provisions supported by the United States are included in the TPP agreement. Some of the possible provisions on government procurement and state-owned enterprises are viewed by some Malaysians as unacceptable infringement on Malaysia's sovereignty and its system of ethnic preferences. Finally, opposition politicians have strongly criticized the government for a lack of transparency in pursuing the negotiations. Under Malaysian law, a TPP agreement, if concluded, must be approved by the Cabinet, with Parliament able to question government ministers on issues addressed in the agreement.

Other Trade Issues

While the TPP negotiations are the main focus at present, other issues also affect trade relations between Malaysia and the United States. The United States has had concerns about Malaysia's IPR protection and would like greater market access for U.S. exports. USTR placed Malaysia on its Special 301 Watch List in 2000 for allegedly inadequate IPR protection, but removed it in 2011. In addition, according to USTR, Malaysia's tariffs and other restrictions on the import of automobiles, automobile parts, and agricultural goods (e.g., regulations on halal food) exceed international norms and restrict U.S. trade with Malaysia. Finally, Malaysia maintains limits on foreign ownership in certain sectors (for example, architectural, engineering, and financial services), as well as licensing and registration restrictions that block greater access for U.S. companies and individuals.[12]

Malaysia will assume the chair of ASEAN in 2015, during which the 10 ASEAN members are to finalize their ASEAN Economic Community (AEC) agreement and the 16 nations negotiating the Regional Comprehensive Economic Partnership (RCEP) are supposed to conclude their talks. RCEP is a proposed regional trade agreement among the 10 ASEAN members (Brunei, Burma, Cambodia, Indonesia, Laos, Malaysia, the Philippines, Singapore, Thailand, and Vietnam), plus Australia, China, India, Japan, New Zealand, and South Korea—similar to the proposed TPP. RCEP negotiations are in their initial stages, but the 16 nations involved have set a goal of concluding the agreement by 2015. Some observers perceive RCEP as a competitor to the TPP, and worry that Malaysia and other nations that are a party to both talks will shift their focus to RCEP if the TPP talks stall. USTR has stated that it sees the two trade agreements as complementary and that the United States is not interested in joining the RCEP negotiations at this time.

DOMESTIC POLITICS

Malaysia has enjoyed a high degree of political stability since it gained independence in 1957. Political coalitions led by the United Malays National Organization (UMNO), the country's dominant political party, have ruled Malaysia without interruption since independence. The present coalition is known as Barisan Nasional (BN, or National Front). Each of Malaysia's seven Prime Ministers has been a member of UMNO, a Malay-nationalist party that draws its membership from the country's Malay majority. The head of state is technically the monarch of Malaysia, the *Yang di-Pertuan Agong*, a position that rotates among the sultans of nine Malay states every five years. The monarch's powers are largely ceremonial.

UMNO's position at the center of the ruling coalition reflects the importance of ethnicity, and to a lesser degree religion, in Malaysian politics. In the 1970s, in an effort to reduce tensions between the nation's Muslim Malay majority and minority groups (primarily Chinese and Indian), UMNO leaders implemented the NEP. At the same time, UMNO recruited smaller parties that represented the country's Chinese and Indian communities into the ruling coalition. In the decades since, the question of the NEP's *bumiputra* preferences, and more broadly of ethnic identity, has become one of the defining issues in Malaysian politics.

Over the past two national elections, in 2008 and then 2013, Malaysian politics has become increasingly competitive. The BN coalition failed to win two-thirds of the Parliament's seats in these elections, for the first time. Minority voters in particular shifted their support to opposition parties because of disillusionment with corruption and with the persistence of what many minorities consider to be discriminatory pro-Malay affirmative action policies. The primary opposition coalition is known as the Pakatan Rakyat (PR, or People's Alliance) and consists of three major parties: the Democratic Action Party (DAP), the Parti Keadilan Rakyat (PKR, or Keadilan), and the Parti Islam se-Malaysia (PAS). PR is a loose coalition that represents dramatically different constituencies and policy agendas. The poor fortunes of the ruling coalition's minority-based parties have raised concerns among some Malaysian observers about the potential for growing ethnic polarization in the country.[13]

In May 2013, the BN won nationwide parliamentary elections, but the results were controversial. The BN won only 47% of the popular vote compared with 51% for the opposition coalition, but won 133 out of Parliament's 222 seats—over 60% of the Parliament. Opposition parties alleged that widespread electoral fraud contributed to the BN's victory, and a series of public protests ensued, drawing tens of thousands of people to several protests in Kuala Lumpur. Some political observers believe the ruling coalition's performance in the elections has weakened Prime Minister Najib's political position, and therefore Najib may take a cautious stance on controversial economic reforms and foreign policy initiatives, such as the TPP.[14]

Malaysia's political landscape is marked by several obstacles to achieving a more robust democracy. Uneven election districting has long elevated the importance of rural electoral districts, and Malaysian election laws require that the states of East Malaysia also retain disproportionate numbers of parliamentary seats—both of which work to UMNO's advantage, as many of these districts are UMNO strongholds. Opposition leaders frequently face government harassment and legal action that many allege is intended to be defamatory.[15]

The position of opposition leader Anwar Ibrahim is of particular sensitivity in Malaysia, and in U.S.-Malaysia relations. From 1993 to 1998, Anwar was the country's Deputy Prime Minister, a UMNO member who was widely considered the heir apparent to longtime Prime Minister Mahathir. After a public break with Mahathir in 1998, Anwar was arrested and accused of sodomy, a crime under Malaysian law. In response to the accusations and evidence of abuse in detention, in October 1998 the U.S. Senate passed S.Res. 294, which called on the Malaysian government to hold a fair trial for Anwar and to preserve the right to express political views freely. U.S. government officials and many international groups criticized the subsequent trial as politically motivated, but Anwar was convicted in 1999 and remained in prison until 2004, when Malaysia's Supreme Court overturned the conviction. He subsequently became the most prominent figure in the country's political opposition. In 2008, Anwar was arrested again for a separate sodomy charge. He was acquitted of the charge in 2012, but, in March 2014 Malaysia's highest appeal court overturned the acquittal and reinstated the charge, sentencing him to five years in prison and potentially costing him the chance to stand in an important state election.

International human rights groups long have criticized other aspects of Malaysia's human rights record. The State Department's 2013 Country Report on Human Rights Practices reported, "The most significant human rights problems included obstacles preventing opposition parties from competing on equal terms with the ruling coalition; restrictions on freedoms of speech, assembly, association, and religion; and restrictions on freedom of the press, including media bias, book banning, censorship, and the denial of printing permits."[16] The State Department gave Malaysia a poor rating (Tier 2 Watch List) in the 2013 Trafficking in Persons report, which noted that the country is home to more than 2 million undocumented foreign laborers.[17]

The Najib government has taken some incremental steps to reduce restrictions on freedom of expression. In September 2011, Najib announced that Malaysia's longstanding Internal Security Act (ISA) would be repealed. Seven months later, in April 2012, Parliament passed a new law called the Security Offenses (Special Measures) 2012 Act (SOSMA), which relaxed some of the ISA's provisions, stating that "no person shall be arrested or detained … solely for his political belief or political activity" and limiting the period individuals can be detained by police without formal charge. However, SOSMA toughened other provisions; for example, allowing police to intercept communications without judicial approval. Human rights groups have criticized the new measures as still overly restrictive.[18]

Malaysia's Diplomacy and Regional Relations

Malaysia harbors a strong self-image as one of Southeast Asia's regional leaders, and as a moderate, Muslim-majority state that can be a political and economic model for others in the Islamic world. It also has been a mediator in seeking to resolve some regional conflicts, most prominently peace talks between the Philippine government and a separatist group in the southern Philippines.

Malaysia was one of the six founding members of ASEAN, Southeast Asia's primary multilateral forum, and it has been a steady proponent of the consensus-based model for regional coordination. Kuala Lumpur was chosen to chair ASEAN in 2015, the year the body hopes to complete the proposed ASEAN Economic Community agreement to strengthen trade and investment bonds. Malaysia is active in many ASEAN initiatives, including the ASEAN Defense Ministers Meeting-Plus (ADMM+), where it worked with Australia as co-chairs of a multilateral maritime security exercise in September 2013.

Among other important issues for Malaysia in its relations with neighboring countries are managing relations with Singapore, with which Malaysia has a deep economic interdependency; dealing with the sometimes-violent separatist movement active in southern Thailand, along Thailand's borders with Malaysia; combatting piracy in the Straits of Malacca along with Indonesia and Singapore; repelling Philippine armed groups that claim parts of Malaysian territory in Sabah; and managing immigration and migrant labor communities from Indonesia, Burma, and other neighbors.

South China Sea Maritime Disputes

Malaysia is one of four Southeast Asian nations with maritime territorial disputes with China (the others are Brunei, the Philippines, and Vietnam). It generally has pursued a less forceful diplomatic approach with China than have the Philippines and Vietnam, and it has sought to have all parties agree to a Code of Conduct to manage behavior in disputed waters. Negotiations between ASEAN's 10 members and China over such a code began in September 2013. Chinese claims in the South China Sea overlap with the Exclusive Economic Zone (EEZ) to which Malaysia is entitled under international law, including the U.N. Convention on the Law of the Sea. Malaysia's own claims also overlap with territorial claims made by the Philippines, Vietnam, and Taiwan.

Because Malaysia is farther geographically from China than the Philippines and Vietnam, incidents at sea between its vessels and vessels from China comparatively are less frequent than Sino-Philippine or Sino-Vietnam incidents. However, in 2013 and 2014 Chinese naval vessels operating as far south as James Shoal, about 50 miles north of the Malaysian coast in Borneo, raised concerns in Malaysia that Chinese territorial assertions in Malaysian-claimed waters may grow more frequent. Observers note that Malaysian economic interests in the South China Sea—particularly in oil and gas development—are considerable. Chinese maritime law enforcement vessels reportedly have interfered with the operation of vessels operated or contracted by Malaysia's state energy company Petronas.[19]

Over the past decade, Malaysia regularly has sought to foster more cooperation among Southeast Asian claimants in efforts to resolve their own disputes and to bolster their claims in disputes with China. For example, in 2007 Malaysia joined Vietnam in submitting a joint extended continental shelf claim to the U.N. Commission on the Limits of the Continental Shelf—a submission that China formally protested. Malaysia's maritime territorial dispute with Brunei was resolved when the two countries signed a boundary agreement in April 2009, facilitated by a subsequent agreement between Petronas and the Brunei government to develop energy blocks off Borneo Island. Some observers describe the agreement as a potential model for utilizing joint development as a means to resolve territorial disputes.[20]

Security Cooperation

The Malaysian military participates in a variety of cooperative security activities on a bilateral and multilateral basis with partners from Southeast Asia and outside the region. Malaysia is a member of the Five-Power Defense Arrangement (FPDA), an agreement between Malaysia, Australia, New Zealand, Singapore, and the United Kingdom to coordinate for mutual defense. The Malaysian and Singaporean militaries cooperate very closely. Malaysia periodically conducts bilateral military exercises with its larger neighbors, China and India. Through the ASEAN-led security groupings—the ASEAN Regional Forum (ARF), the ASEAN Defense Ministers' Meeting (ADMM), and the ADDM Plus—Malaysia has participated actively in regional security dialogues and cooperative activities. As an example of the potential for conflict avoidance mechanisms in the region, in 2013 Malaysia and Vietnam agreed to establish a "direct connection" communication link between a Malaysian naval base and Vietnam's Southern Command.[21] In the Straits of Malacca, the Malaysian military and maritime law enforcement work closely with counterparts from Singapore and Indonesia on anti-piracy measures that have considerably lessened the incidence of piracy in the heavily traveled waters over the past decade.

The Mysterious Disappearance of Flight MH370: What Did We Learn?

In the early morning hours of March 8, 2014, Malaysia Airlines Flight MH370, flying from Kuala Lumpur to Beijing, ceased normal communication with air traffic controllers and deviated from its course. The path of the missing aircraft was uncertain for more than a week after its disappearance. Eventually, data from military radar in the area and from satellites operated by the British company Inmarsat determined the flight's likely trajectory: the aircraft appeared to have veered west over the Malay Peninsula and then flew south over the Indian Ocean. Malaysian authorities announced on March 24 that the flight "ended in the southern Indian Ocean;" the crew and 239 passengers presumably died.[22] As of mid-April 2014, there was no clear cause for the diversion of Flight MH370 and its presumed crash into the ocean.

In the international and Malaysian reporting on the plane's disappearance, several narratives emerged that attempt to draw broader conclusions from this incident. Critics of the Najib government argue that the Malaysian authorities performed poorly in this crisis and displayed an endemic inefficiency, poor coordination, paternalism, and incompetence.[23] Defenders of the government's performance point out that the case of Flight MH370 was uniquely complex and that few governments have the capacity for handling such an incident.[24]

The need for international cooperation in locating the missing aircraft showcased both the strengths and weaknesses of cooperative efforts in the Asia-Pacific region. On one hand, observers (in China, especially) criticized the Malaysian government for being too slow to share information and for being unwilling to reveal data from military sources.[25] The ad hoc response from the international community showed the limits of existing international organizations to handle such an incident. On the other hand, many countries contributed military and civilian resources to locating the plane and coordinated their search efforts.[26]

The United States assisted Malaysia in several aspects of the response. FBI agents aided in the investigations of passengers and crew in Malaysia. Officials from the National Transportation Safety Board (NTSB), along with technical advisers from Boeing and the Federal Aviation Administration (FAA), helped to determine the trajectory of Flight MH370. The U.S. military mobilized a number of ships and aircraft, including highly specialized equipment, to search for the downed plane at a cost of at least $7.3 million through mid-April 2014.[27] A senior U.S. official praised the Malaysian government for its efforts and asserted that the cooperative effort to investigate the plane's disappearance could help to build bilateral ties.[28]

Conflict Mediation and Promotion of Moderate Islam

Malaysia promotes itself as a leading voice for moderate Muslim countries; Kuala Lumpur maintains good relations with the United States and other Western countries while speaking out for Islamic causes, such as the status of the Palestinians. Malaysia is an active participant in the Organization of Islamic Conferences (OIC), and even has launched its own initiative, the

Global Movement of Moderates (GMM), to diminish extremist voices and improve the public image of Muslims worldwide.

Within Southeast Asia, Malaysia has played an active role as a mediator in conflicts between rebel Muslim groups and the central government in both Thailand and in the Philippines. Malaysia helped to broker a 2014 peace agreement between Manila and the Moro Islamic Liberation Front (MILF), a group that seeks more autonomy for the Muslim minority in the southern Philippines.

U.S.-MALAYSIA SECURITY RELATIONS

In a 2002 speech in Washington, DC, then-Defense Minister Najib Razak called the cooperative U.S.-Malaysia defense relationship "an all too well-kept secret."[29] Despite discord at the political leadership level, the United States and Malaysia have maintained a steady level of defense cooperation since the 1990s, and several aspects of that cooperation improved in the 2010s as the overall relationship warmed. The Obama Administration's strategic rebalancing to the Asia-Pacific region has put more emphasis on bolstering security ties with Malaysia and other so-called "emerging partners."

During the 2000s, a major focus of U.S.-Malaysia security cooperation was counter-terrorism activities aimed at terrorist networks operating in Southeast Asia.[30] Malaysia itself has not been a base for major terrorist or insurgent groups, but it played a central role as a moderate Muslim voice against terrorism and as a capacity-building partner, establishing the Southeast Asia Regional Centre for Counter-Terrorism in 2003. Based on a 2002 bilateral Memorandum of Understanding on counter-terrorism, the law enforcement and intelligence communities of the United States and Malaysia also have enhanced their cooperation in areas such as tracking financial flows. In FY2013 and FY2014, the United States provided Malaysia with $2 million in assistance through the International Narcotics Control and Law Enforcement (INCLE) program and the Nonproliferation, Anti-Terrorist, Demining and Related Programs (NADR).

The U.S. and Malaysian defense establishments have built solid ties through frequent military exercises, combined training, ship visits, and military education exchanges. Every year, dozens of Malaysian officers study at U.S. professional military education institutions through International Military Education and Training (IMET) programs. The United States and Malaysia jointly fund these exchanges to build interpersonal connections and to improve the professionalism of the Malaysian military. In 2013, the U.S. and Malaysian militaries conducted over 75 cooperative activities, highlighted by jungle warfare training at a Malaysian facility, bilateral exercises like Kris Strike, and multilateral exercises like Cobra Gold, which is held in Thailand and involves thousands of personnel from several Asian countries plus the United States. Since 2010, Malaysia has participated in the biennial "Rim of the Pacific" (RIMPAC) multilateral naval exercises held near Hawaii. U.S. military vessels dock at ports in Malaysia for re-supply, for maintenance, and to allow U.S. servicemembers to build ties with their Malaysian counterparts.

As the number of U.S. ship visits to Malaysia rose from single digits in the early 2000s, to 10s of visits in the late 2000s, and then to more than 30 visits in 2011, the U.S. Navy began to investigate the suspicious port-hosting contracts of a Malaysian businessman, Leonard Glenn Francis. In 2013, the Navy concluded that Francis's company, Glenn Defense Marine Asia (Glenn Marine), had bribed high-ranking American officers and bilked the Navy out of tens of millions of dollars.[31] The Glenn Marine scandal led to the investigation of two admirals and a Navy-wide review of similar supply contracts around the world.

U.S.-Malaysia security cooperation extends around the world, to include peacekeeping, counter-piracy, and reconstruction operations. As mentioned above, from 2010 until 2013 Malaysia deployed a contingent of 40 military medical personnel to Afghanistan, where they made contributions to public health (especially women's health) and clean water access. The U.S. and Malaysian navies cooperate to combat piracy near the Malacca Strait and, as part of the international counter-piracy coalition, off the Horn ofAfrica. Malaysia is a large contributor to U.N. peacekeeping operations, and has roughly 900 personnel serving in several missions, as of April 2014. In December 2013, Malaysia became the first country to complete the peacekeeping training program run by the U.S. State Department's Office of the Global Peace Operations Initiative.

Malaysia has purchased high-technology U.S. weapons systems in the past, notably the F/A-18D Hornet strike fighter aircraft, but its recent major defense purchases mostly have been of European equipment. The most modern Malaysian fighter aircraft is the Russian Su-30MKM Flanker, and the French "Scorpene" design won the contract for Malaysia's only two submarines. The Malaysian defense budget for FY2013 was $4.72 billion. Reportedly, U.S. defense firms are interested in establishing close partnerships with their Malaysian counterparts to cooperate in military procurement.[32]

Outlook

Many observers believe that, in the near term, bilateral U.S.-Malaysia relations may benefit from the same factors that have produced warmer ties in recent years: Prime Minister Najib's relatively pro-American alignment and the Obama Administration's rebalancing strategy. President Obama's April 2014 visit to Malaysia could boost the relationship somewhat, although expectations are low for tangible policy outcomes. The main policy challenge for Washington and Kuala Lumpur in the immediate future will be the TPP negotiations. The result of the negotiations and the domestic process of ratification, in which Congress would play a key role, will be a major factor in defining the overall state of U.S.-Malaysia relations.

The future of domestic politics in Malaysia is difficult to forecast with confidence. The ruling BN coalition no longer has a stranglehold on political power, but the opposition coalition PR has been unable to gain a parliamentary majority in the last two national elections. The distribution of seats in favor of rural constituencies and the deference of the mainstream press to government narratives will continue to favor the UMNO-led coalition. On the other hand, dissatisfaction with government inefficiency and corruption could give the opposition enough popular support to capture a majority in the next elections, which must be held by 2018. The government's treatment of Anwar Ibrahim runs the risk that it could engender more sympathy for the opposition leader and could backfire on UMNO in the long run.

Many observers believe the NEP's set of ethnic preferences also will be a key issue for Malaysia in the years ahead. Although the NEP has been given some credit in addressing Malaysia's income disparities and maintaining peaceful relations among ethnic groups, it also has fostered resentment among Malaysia's Chinese and Indian minorities. The NEP policies favoring *bumiputra*-owned domestic companies in government hindered earlier FTA negotiations with the United States. However, many analysts see the NEP as a bedrock of the Malaysian political economy and believe that any move strongly to scale back preferences for *bumiputra* would face deep opposition from many members of the Malay ethnic majority.

Prime Minister Mahathir long promoted a "Vision 2020," which sought to make Malaysia into a developed country by that year, and the 2020 goal has been taken up by subsequent UMNO-led governments. Although Malaysia's GDP has grown steadily in the last decade, rebounding quickly from the 2008-2009 global financial crisis, several challenges remain. Within Southeast Asia and worldwide, Malaysia faces stiff competition from other low-wage countries attempting to promote their manufacturing sectors and grow exports. Some observers argue that the quality of the education system is not sufficient for development of a high-technology economy. Many of Malaysia's top students go abroad for higher education, or find work overseas after graduation, a phenomenon known as "brain drain." At the same time, the TPP and RCEP trade agreements could be an opportunity to grow the Malaysian economy through expanded trade.

Many of Malaysia's challenges in the years ahead will mirror those of other Southeast Asian nations. Like others in ASEAN, Malaysia continually seeks to balance the involvement of the United States, China, Japan, India, and others in regional affairs, while maintaining its own independence and that of ASEAN broadly. Malaysia competes with other Southeast Asian nations as an exporter and as a destination for foreign investment, but Southeast Asia as a region also competes with other parts of the world. SoutheastAsian nations must decide how deeply to proceed with economic integration aimed at promoting a broader regional trading and investment hub. As ASEAN's chair in 2015, the organization's target year for completing an ASEAN Economic Community, Malaysia will face challenges in balancing the region's trade and investment agendas, while also providing leadership on regional security issues such as lowering tensions in the South China Sea.

End Notes

[1] Other CRS products cover issues related to Malaysia. These include CRS Report R42694, *The Trans-Pacific Partnership (TPP) Negotiations and Issues for Congress*, coordinated by Ian F. Fergusson, CRS Report R42344, *Trans-Pacific Partnership (TPP) Countries: Comparative Trade and Economic Analysis*, by Brock R. Williams, and CRS Report R42930, *Maritime Territorial Disputes in East Asia: Issues for Congress* , by Ben Dolven, Shirley A. Kan, and Mark E. Manyin. Archived reports include CRS Report RL33445, *The Proposed U.S.-Malaysia Free Trade Agreement*, by Michael F. Martin, CRS Report RL33878, *U.S.-Malaysia Relations: Implications of the 2008 Elections*, by Michael F. Martin, and CRS Report RL34194, *Terrorism in Southeast Asia*, coordinated by Bruce Vaughn.

[2] Joshua Kurlantzick, "Obama in Malaysia: A Strategic Partnership?" Council on Foreign Relations, Asia Unbound blog, April 8, 2014.

[3] Jen Psaki, "Conviction of Malaysian Opposition Leader Anwar Ibrahim," U.S. Department of State, Washington, DC, March 7, 2014, http://www.state.gov/r/pa/prs/ps/2014/03/ 223148.htm.

[4] Patrick Ventrell, U.S. Department of State Daily Press Briefing, Washington, DC, May 6, 2013, http://www.state.gov/ r/pa/prs/dpb/2013/05/208988.htm#Malaysia.

[5] The discrepancy between the official Malaysian and U.S. trade statistics is not unusual. The United States evaluates its exports and imports differently from most other nations, but the methods of accounting are equally accurate.

[6] For more about the TPP negotiations, see CRS Report R42694, *The Trans-Pacific Partnership (TPP) Negotiations and Issues for Congress*, coordinated by Ian F. Fergusson.

[7] Australia, Peru, and Vietnam joined the TPP talks in 2008. Mexico and Canada joined in 2012, and Japan in 2013. Under an agreement among the negotiating nations, a new member cannot join the negotiations unless it gains consent from all the current parties to the talks.

[8] Penny Pritzker, "America's Economic Future in the Asia-Pacific," remarks as delivered at the Johns Hopkins University School of Advanced International Studies, Washington, DC, April 17, 2014.

[9] For more information about the bilateral trade talks, see CRS Report RL33445, *The Proposed U.S.-Malaysia Free Trade Agreement*, by Michael F. Martin.

[10] "Malaysia Flags Major TPP Outstanding Issues, Says U.S. Needs TPA to Close," *Inside U.S. Trade*, February 28, 2014.

[11] "45 State Attorneys General Call for Tobacco Carve Out in the TPP", Action on Smoking & Health website, January 28, 2014, http://ash.org/45-state-attorneys-general-call-for-tobacco-carve-out-in-the-tpp.

[12] "2014 National Trade Estimate Report on Foreign Trade Barriers," Office of the United States Trade Representative, Washington, DC, March 2014.

[13] Huihui Ooi, "What's Next, Malaysia?" Atlantic Council, The New Atlanticist blog, May 16, 2013, http://www.atlanticcouncil.org/blogs/new-atlanticist/whats-next-malaysia.

[14] Jeremy Grant, "Knives out for Malaysia PM Najib Razak," *Financial Times*, February 5, 2014.

[15] "Malaysia: Anwar Ibrahim Decision 'A Bleak Day for Justice'," Amnesty International, March 7, 2014.

[16] 2013 Country Report on Human Rights Practices: Malaysia, U.S. Department of State, Washington, DC, February 27, 2014, http://www.state.gov/j/drl/rls/hrrpt/2013/eap/220209.htm.

[17] Trafficking in Persons Report 2013, U.S. Department of State, Washington, DC, June 19, 2013.

[18] See Human Rights Watch, *Smoke and Mirrors: Malaysia's "New" Internal Security Act.* June 19, 2012.

[19] Carlyle A. Thayer, "Can ASEAN Rise to the Chinese Challenge?" Yale Global Online. March 18, 2014.

[20] See, for instance, Clive Schofield, "Maritime Energy Resources in Asia: Legal Regimes and Cooperation," National Bureau of Asian Research, February 2012.

[21] "Malaysia boosts its regional defense cooperation," *United Press International*, November 1, 2013.

[22] "Transcript of Malaysian Prime Minister Najib Razak's statement on flight MH370," *Associated Press*, March 24, 2014.

[23] Hui Mei Liew Kaiser, "Tall Stories," *Foreign Policy*, March 25, 2014.

[24] "Tough for Malaysia if foreign govts slow to react or not forthcoming with info," *Star* (Malaysia), March 20, 2014

[25] Gordon Lubold, "The Fear of Sharing and the Search for Flight 370," *Foreign Policy*, March 30, 2014.

[26] Santha Oorjitham, "Missing MH370: Unprecedented level of cooperation," *Star* (Malaysia), March 21, 2014.

[27] For more information on U.S. military participation in the search for flight MH370, see the U.S. Defense Department website, "Navy Assists Search for Malaysian Airliner," http://www.defense.gov/home/features/2014/0314_flight370.

[28] Yoichi Kato, "INTERVIEW/ Evan Medeiros: China's attempt to isolate Japan worsens bilateral relations," *Asahi Shimbun,* April 6, 2014.

[29] Najib bin Abdul Razak, "U.S.-Malaysia Defense Cooperation: A Solid Success Story," remarks as prepared for delivery at the Heritage Foundation, Washington, DC, May 3, 2002.

[30] For more information, see CRS Report RL34194, *Terrorism in Southeast Asia*, coordinated by Bruce Vaughn.

[31] Christopher Drew and Danielle Ivory, "Navy Was Warned of Contractor at Center of Bribery Inquiry," *New York Times*, November 20, 2013.

[32] Andrew Shapiro, "U.S.-Malaysia Partnership," remarks as prepared for delivery at Malaysia Armed Forces Defense College, Kuala Lumpur, Malaysia, February 15, 2012.

In: Malaysia
Editor: Paulina Collins

ISBN: 978-1-63321-227-5

Chapter 2

MALAYSIA 2013 HUMAN RIGHTS REPORT*

U.S. Department of State; Bureau of Democracy, Human Rights and Labor

EXECUTIVE SUMMARY

Malaysia is a federal constitutional monarchy. It has a parliamentary system of government selected through periodic, multi-party elections and headed by a prime minister. The king is the head of state and serves a largely ceremonial role; the kingship rotates among the nine sultans every five years. The United Malays National Organization (UMNO), together with a coalition of political parties known as the National Front (BN), has held power since independence in 1957. On May 5, in general elections, the BN was re-elected although it lost the popular vote to the opposition coalition. The opposition and civil society organizations alleged electoral irregularities. Civilian authorities failed at times to maintain effective control over security forces. Security forces committed human rights abuses.

The most significant human rights problems included obstacles preventing opposition parties from competing on equal terms with the ruling coalition; restrictions on freedoms of speech, assembly, association, and religion; and

---

* This is an edited, reformatted and augmented version of a report released by the U.S. Department of State; Bureau of Democracy, Human Rights and Labor, dated February 2014.

restrictions on freedom of the press, including media bias, book banning, censorship, and the denial of printing permits.

Other human rights problems included deaths during police apprehension and while in police custody; the persistence of laws that allow detention without trial; caning as a form of punishment imposed by criminal and sharia courts; bans on religious groups; restrictions on proselytizing and on the freedom to change one's religion; official corruption; violence and discrimination against women; discrimination against lesbian, gay, bisexual, and transgender (LGBT) persons; and restrictions on the rights of migrants, including migrant workers, refugees, and victims of human trafficking. Longstanding government policies gave preferences to ethnic Malays in many areas. The government restricted union and collective- bargaining activity, and government policies created vulnerabilities and worsened child labor and forced labor problems, especially for migrant workers.

The government prosecuted some officials engaged in corruption and human rights abuses, although some degree of impunity continued.

SECTION 1. RESPECT FOR THE INTEGRITY OF THE PERSON, INCLUDING FREEDOM FROM

a. Arbitrary or Unlawful Deprivation of Life

There were reports the government or its agents committed arbitrary or unlawful killings. One nongovernmental organization (NGO) reported 49 individuals were killed in police shootings in 2012. The home minister announced that police shot 124 persons from 2009 to August 2013, including 56 Malays, 41 Indians, 23 Chinese, and four indigenous persons. State-influenced media often used a common narrative to describe these encounters: suspect was stopped by police, tried to attack police; police killed suspect in self-defense; and evidence of criminal activity was found on suspect's body. Local human rights groups suggested this narrative was used to justify deaths in the course of arrest or in police custody.

There is no entity that examines security force killings. Investigation into a killing by a law enforcement officer only occurs if the attorney general initiates the investigation, or if he approves an application for an investigation by family members of the deceased. In previous years, when the attorney general has ordered an inquest, a coroner's court was convened and the hearing was open to the public. In these cases, the court has generally issued an open verdict, which meant no verdict was reached, and no further action taken against the police.

On January 18, police shot and killed Pua Bee Chun after she allegedly fled a crime scene as a passenger in a stolen car. Police reportedly fired more than 20 times at the car. In August Chun's family filed a summons to compel authorities to reveal the results of their investigation into the shooting.

On June 26, with regard to the 2009 death in custody of Ananthan Kugan, the high court awarded Kugan's mother Ringgit Malaysia (RM) 851,700 ($260,000) for assault and battery, false imprisonment, misfeasance, and pain and suffering. In 2012 the High Court convicted police constable Vivekanandan Navindran of causing "grievous hurt" to Kugan and sentenced him to three years in prison.

b. Disappearance

There were no reports of politically motivated disappearances.

c. Torture and Other Cruel, Inhuman, or Degrading Treatment or Punishment

No law specifically prohibits torture; however, laws that prohibit "committing grievous hurt" encompass torture.

More than 60 offenses are subject to caning, and judges routinely included caning in sentences of those convicted of such crimes as kidnapping, rape, and robbery, as well as some nonviolent crimes, such as narcotics possession, criminal breach of trust, and alien smuggling. The law also prescribes punishment of up to six strokes of the cane for both illegal immigrants and their employers.

Caning is carried out with a half-inch-thick wooden cane that may cause welts and scarring. The law exempts men older than 50 and all women from caning. Male children between the ages of 10 and 18 may be given up to 10 strokes of a "light cane." The government revealed in a letter to a parliamentarian that from 2010 to June 2013 it caned 42,634 prisoners, of whom 26,214 were Malaysians and 16,420 were foreigners.

Some states' sharia laws-- those governing family issues and certain crimes under Islam and which apply only to Muslims--also prescribe caning for certain offenses. Although federal law exempts all women from caning, there are no exemptions for women under sharia, and the national courts have not yet resolved issues involving conflicts among the constitution, the penal code, and sharia. Sharia caning uses a smaller cane, and the caning official is not supposed to lift the cane above the shoulder, thus reducing the impact. The subject is also fully covered with a robe. Local Islamic officials claimed the objective is not to injure but to make offenders ashamed of their sin so they would repent and not repeat the offense.

Prison and Detention Center Conditions

Prison conditions were harsh, with some deaths of prisoners and detainees, particularly in police holding cells.

Physical Conditions: Prison overcrowding, particularly in facilities near major cities, remained a serious problem. In June the Ministry of Home Affairs reported that the country's 30 prisons held 39,144 prisoners in facilities designed to hold 32,000. According to the International Centre for Prison Studies, in mid-2012 women made up 5.8 percent and juveniles 2.2 percent of the total prison population. Authorities generally held men separately from women, juveniles separately from adults, and pretrial detainees separately from convicted prisoners. Prisons provided potable water.

Local and international NGOs estimated most of the country's 17 immigration detention centers (IDCs) were at or beyond capacity, with some detainees held for a year or more. NGOs and international organizations involved with migrant workers and refugees made credible allegations of overcrowding, inadequate food and clothing, lack of regular access to clean water, poor medical care, improper sanitation, and lack of bedding in IDCs. An NGO with access to the IDCs claimed these conditions and lack of medical screening and treatment facilitated the spread of disease and contributed to continued deaths in IDCs. The government allowed local NGOs to visit IDCs from time to time. NGOs provided most of the medical care and treatment in IDCs.

Accusations of rape of prisoners while in prison or detention occurred.

Death of prisoners while in prison or detention occurred. A local NGO reported that there were seven cases of death in custody from January to June. On May 21, N. Dharmendran died en route to the hospital after complaining of chest pains while in police custody at the Bukit Aman jail where he was detained for 10 days. A government hospital autopsy report surmised that he died from multiple beatings. The lawyer for the family reported Dharmendran's ears were stapled and his back and legs had marks of physical abuse. Four police officers were implicated in the death and awaited trial at year's end.

On January 23, C. Sugumaran died in police custody in Hulu Langat district, Selangor state. Eyewitnesses reported members of the public and police beat Sugumaran to death after he was chased by police and handcuffed. An initial autopsy concluded Sugumaran died of a heart attack; however, this was disputed by the family. After the prime minister called for an inquest into the death, the Health Ministry ordered another autopsy by an outside pathologist. The case remained open as of October.

In January the Court of Appeal upheld a 2011 ruling to award RM500,000 ($15,290) to the family of Mohd Shukri Mohamed Yusof, an 18-year-old who died in custody in 2004. In 2007 the family filed a civil suit against the prison and the government for wrongful death. One warden of the prison was sentenced to death for the murder of Mohd Shukri.

On August 13, a pathologist reported to the coroner's court that foul play was unlikely in the August 2012 death of Cheah Chin Lee. Cheah died at the Tanjung Tokong Police Headquarters in Penang five hours after his arrest for theft. According to news reports the Penang Hospital attributed his death to "asphyxia due to hanging," but his family doubted that he would commit suicide and filed a police report. The case remained open at year's end.

In July Home Minister Ahmad Zahid Hamidi announced that there were 231 cases of custodial deaths from 2000 to May 2013; he stated that most deaths were due to natural causes. He maintained that only two of the deaths were caused by police.

Administration: NGOs considered recordkeeping adequate. Authorities did not use alternatives to imprisonment for nonviolent offenders. Prisoners and detainees are allowed visitors during specified visiting hours, and, freedom of religious observance provided religious practices were not derived from one of the sects of Islam the government bans as "deviant." The Prisons Act does not provide a process for prisoners to submit complaints to judicial authorities, but it allows judges to visit prisons to examine conditions and ask prisoners and prison officials about prison conditions. The Human Rights Commission of Malaysia (SUHAKAM) serves as the government's de facto ombudsman, investigating allegations of human rights abuses within the prison system. According to local NGOs, because prison authorities reportedly monitored all incoming and outgoing materials, complaints normally would not be sent through prison authorities. Communications between an attorney and his or her client generally were treated as private and confidential under the attorney-client privilege.

Independent Monitoring: Authorities generally did not permit NGOs and the media to monitor prison conditions. The government approved visits by the International Committee of the Red Cross and SUHAKAM officials on a case-by- case basis.

The UN High Commissioner for Refugees (UNHCR) had access to registered refugees, asylum seekers, and unregistered persons of concern who may have claims to asylum and refugee status and are detained in IDCs and prisons. The UNHCR conducted 203 missions to detention facilities and secured the release of 6,351 refugees from IDCs from January through October.

Although the Internal Security Act (ISA) was repealed and replaced with the Security Offenses (Special Measures) Act in 2012, the law allows existing detainees to be held at the home minister's discretion. At year's end, six ISA detainees remained in custody.

d. Arbitrary Arrest or Detention

The constitution stipulates that no person may be incarcerated unless in accordance with the law. The law, however, allows investigative detention to prevent a criminal suspect from fleeing or destroying evidence during an investigation. On October 2, parliament passed the Prevention of Crime (Amendment and Extension) Bill (PCA), which extended the possible term of detention without trial under that law from 72 days to two years and made the term renewable. The legislation transferred authority for ordering such detentions from the minister of home affairs to a five-person Prevention of Crime Board. A suspect brought before the board is not entitled to legal representation. The amended law provides that detention without trial could be invoked for certain registered persons. The Home Ministry may register persons suspected of involvement in organized crime or previously convicted of crimes involving dishonesty or violence. The law requires the home minister to submit an annual report on the implementation of these authorities and provides that these authorities will expire in five years unless renewed by parliament. Civil society organizations and the parliamentary opposition expressed concern that the law could be misused for political purposes.

In 2012 parliament passed the Security Offenses (Special Measures) Act (SOSMA) along with amendments to the penal code, the Criminal Procedure Code, and the Evidence Act. The SOSMA focuses on terrorism and other national security crimes and stipulates that once an arrest has been made, the next of kin must be notified immediately and the accused must have access to a lawyer within 24 hours. A high-ranking police officer may extend the detention period to 28 days, at which time the accused must be charged or released. The law also states that a person may not be charged for his political beliefs or activities. NGO observers criticized what they see as vague language in the SOSMA, such as activities "detrimental to parliamentary democracy" or "activity…that is prejudicial to the security or interest of Malaysia," and the ability of police to extend detention within the 28-day period without judicial review. Additionally, some observers criticized provisions that allow the identity of witnesses to be kept secret, inhibiting cross-examination of witnesses, and allowing the accused to be kept in detention after an acquittal if the prosecution decides to appeal.

The Dangerous Drugs Act gives the government specific power to detain suspected drug traffickers without trial for up to 39 days before the home affairs minister must issue a detention order. Once the ministry issues the detention order, the detainee is entitled to a hearing before a court, which has the authority to order the detainee's release. Authorities may hold suspects without charge for successive two-year intervals with periodic review by an advisory board, whose opinion is binding on the minister. Police sometimes detained suspected narcotics traffickers under this act after formal charges were not pursued.

The Immigration Act also allows authorities to arrest and detain noncitizens for 30 days pending a decision on deportation; deportation orders cannot be appealed.

Under the terms of the government's antitrafficking legislation, foreign trafficking victims certified under a protection order were forced to remain in the country during court proceedings of their cases, and were detained in government facilities for the duration of the trials against their traffickers.

Role of the Police and Security Apparatus

The approximately 102,000-member Royal Malaysia Police (RMP) force is under the command of the inspector general of police who reports to the home affairs minister. The inspector general of police is responsible for organizing and administering the police force. The Malaysia Department of

Islamic Development (JAKIM) enforces sharia, which applies only to Muslims, in Kuala Lumpur and the federal territories. JAKIM sometimes receives assistance from the RMP when conducting raids. State-level Islamic religious enforcement officers also have the authority to accompany police on raids or conduct raids of private premises as well as public establishments to enforce sharia, including violations such as indecent dress, alcohol consumption, selling of banned books, or close proximity to members of the opposite sex. Religious authorities at the state level administer sharia through Islamic courts and have jurisdiction over all Muslims. Sharia and the degree of its enforcement vary by state, and the penalties imposed by sharia courts are limited under the civil law.

The People's Volunteer Corps (RELA) is a paramilitary civilian volunteer corps under the jurisdiction of the Ministry of Home Affairs. The Malaysian Volunteer Corps Act of 2012 describes the main duty of RELA as to "assist any security force or authority established under written law upon request of the force or authority" and stipulates that, while performing those duties, RELA members will be "under the command of an officer of the security force or authority…who is present at the place."

As of September RELA membership stood at 2.9 million. According to a statement by RELA Director General Mustafa Ibrahim, RELA members undergo two training courses. The first is an introductory course; the second is a seven-day basic training course in which trainees are taught discipline, human rights and integrity, and handling arms in cases of emergency. RELA members serve at IDCs, customs and immigration quarantine complexes, national borders, airports in Sabah and Sarawak, and gas stations in border towns to prevent fuel smuggling.

RELA members also monitor 400 schools nationwide. NGOs remained concerned that inadequate training left RELA members ill equipped to perform their duties. Reported abuses by RELA members included extortion, theft, pilfering items from homes, and pillaging of refugee housing. Reports of abuse, however, were fewer than in previous years.

The government did not release information on how it investigated complaints against RELA members or how it administered disciplinary action. The Public Protection Authorities Act of 1948 and a 2005 Amendment to Essential Regulations give RELA members legal immunity for official acts committed in good faith.

The government has some mechanisms to investigate and punish abuse and corruption, and SUHAKAM played a role in investigating alleged abuses committed by the security forces. There were NGO and media reports security forces acted with impunity.

Police officers are subject to trial by the criminal and civil courts. Police representatives reported there were disciplinary actions against police officers and that punishment included suspension, dismissal, and demotion.

An independent police complaints and misconduct commission had yet to be established by year's end.

The police training center included human rights awareness training in its courses. SUHAKAM also conducted human rights training and workshops for police and prison officials.

The Enforcement Agency Integrity Commission announced that from its inception in April 2011 through May 2013 it received 469 complaints of abuse. Of these, 353 involved the RMP. There were also complaints regarding RELA and officers of the Immigration Department. In June the then chief executive of the commission told the media that her organization had insufficient resources, with only one investigating officer to probe complaints against 19 enforcement agencies. Shortly after, she was transferred back to the attorney general's chambers with no replacement appointed.

Arrest Procedures and Treatment of Detainees

The law permits police to arrest individuals for some offenses without a warrant. Under SOSMA, a suspect may be held for 24 hours, which may be extended up to 28 days on the authority of a police superintendent, but then the suspect must be brought before a magistrate or released. Under the PCA, a Prevention of Crime Board may order certain suspects to be detained without trial for up to two years. Although police generally observed these provisions, local NGOs reported the police practice of releasing suspects and then quickly re-arresting and holding them in investigative custody continued. Some NGOs asserted a police approach of "arrest first, investigate later" was prevalent. By law an arrested individual has the right to be informed of the grounds for arrest by the arresting police officer.

Bail is usually available for those accused of crimes not punishable by life imprisonment or death. The amount and availability of bail is determined at the judge's discretion. When bail is granted, accused persons usually must surrender their passports to the court.

Police must inform detainees that they are allowed to contact family members and consult a lawyer of their choice. Police often denied detainees access to legal counsel and questioned suspects without giving them access to counsel. Police justified this practice as necessary to prevent interference in ongoing investigations, and judicial decisions generally upheld the practice. On some occasions law enforcement agencies did not promptly allow access to family members.

The law allows the detention of a material witness in a criminal case if that person is likely to flee.

Arbitrary Arrest: More than 100 people were detained under SOSMA, most in connection with the incursion by militants from the southern Philippines into Sabah. Thirty people, including 29 men and one woman, who were arrested for either invading Sabah or aiding and abetting those who did, awaited a hearing at year's end.

From January to June of 2012, the government detained 433 persons under the preventive detention provisions of the Dangerous Drugs (Special Preventive Measures) Act. During the same time period, according to the Anti-Drug Enforcement Agency, 61,584 people were arrested for drug related offenses and the National Anti-Narcotics Agency identified 4,760 new drug addicts, compared with 11,194 in 2011 and 23,642 in 2010, of whom 3,136 were considered "youths."

Pretrial Detention: Crowded and understaffed courts often resulted in lengthy pretrial detention, sometimes lasting several years. The International Center for Prison Studies reported that as of mid-2012, pretrial detainees made up 21.6 percent of the total prisoner population.

Detention of Rejected Asylum Seekers or Stateless Persons: A rejected Sri Lanka asylum seeker died of leptospirosis in Seremban Hospital after he became ill while in the Lenggeng immigration detention center.

e. Denial of Fair Public Trial

Three constitutional articles provide the basis for an independent judiciary; however, other constitutional provisions, legislation restricting judicial review, and additional factors limited judicial independence and strengthened executive influence over the judiciary.

Members of the bar, NGO representatives, and other observers expressed serious concern about significant limitations on judicial independence, citing a number of high-profile instances of arbitrary verdicts, selective prosecution, and preferential treatment of some litigants and lawyers.

In 2012 parliamentary opposition leader Anwar Ibrahim was acquitted on charges of having engaged in consensual sodomy in 2008. The attorney general's chambers filed an appeal of the acquittal five months later during the same year. Hearings on the substance of the appeal were pending at year's end.

Trial Procedures

English common law is the basis for the secular legal system. The constitution states that all persons are equal before the law and entitled to equal protection of the law. Defendants are presumed innocent until proven guilty. Trials are public, although judges may order restrictions on press coverage. Juries are not used. Defendants have the right to counsel at public expense if facing charges that may carry the death penalty and may apply for a public defender in certain other cases. According to the Bar Council, defendants generally have adequate time and facilities to prepare a defense if they have the means to engage private counsel. Otherwise the defendants must rely on legal aid and the amount of time to prepare for the trial is at the discretion of the judge. Strict rules of evidence apply in court; however, government-held evidence was not consistently made available to the defense. Defendants confronted witnesses against them and presented witnesses and evidence on their behalf, although judges sometimes disallowed witness testimony. Defendants may make statements for the record to an investigative agency prior to trial. Limited pretrial discovery in criminal cases impeded defendants' ability to defend themselves. Attorneys must apply for a court order to obtain documents covered under the Official Secrets Act. Defendants may appeal court decisions to higher courts, but the law limits a defendant's right to appeal in instances where the appeal does not raise a question of law and the evidence is sufficient to support the conviction or no material on the circumstances of the case would raise a reasonable doubt of the conviction or that the sentence should be reduced. The government stated that the limits expedite the hearing of cases in the upper courts, but the Bar Council declared that they impose excessive restrictions on appeals.

In firearm and certain national security cases, a lower standard is in effect for accepting self-incriminating statements by defendants as evidence.

Many NGOs complained that women did not receive fair treatment from sharia courts, especially in matters of divorce and child custody.

Political Prisoners and Detainees

There were no reports of political prisoners or detainees. Following the May elections, authorities arrested opposition member of parliament Tian Chua, vice president of the opposition People's Justice Party (PKR); and pro-opposition activists Haris Ibrahim, Tamrin Ghafar, and Adam Adli under the Sedition Act for allegedly attempting to topple the government through street protests. All were free awaiting trial at year's end.

Civil Judicial Procedures and Remedies

The government and officials may be sued in court for alleged violations of human rights. The structure of the civil judiciary mirrors that of the criminal courts. A large case backlog often resulted in delayed court-ordered relief for civil plaintiffs. The courts have increasingly encouraged the use of mediation and arbitration to speed settlements.

f. Arbitrary Interference with Privacy, Family, Home, or Correspondence

Various laws prohibit arbitrary interference with privacy rights; nevertheless, authorities infringed on citizens' privacy rights in some cases. Provisions in the security legislation allow police to enter and search without a warrant the homes of persons suspected of threatening national security. Police also may confiscate evidence under these provisions. Police used this legal authority to search homes and offices; seize computers, books, and newspapers; monitor conversations; and take persons into custody without a warrant. The government monitored e-mails sent to internet blog sites and threatened to detain anyone sending content over the internet that the government deemed threatening to public order or security.

JAKIM guidelines authorize JAKIM officials to enter private premises without a warrant if they deem swift action necessary to catch Muslims suspected of engaging in offenses such as gambling, consumption of alcohol, and sexual relations outside marriage.

On February 14, in what has become an annual occurrence since the issuance of an anti-Valentine's Day fatwa in 2005, officers from the Department of Federal Territory Islamic Affairs arrested 10 Muslim individuals for khalwat (close proximity to a member of the opposite sex) during a Valentine's Day operation. In addition to the 10, the department ordered three Muslim men who were found with non-Muslim women to undergo counseling by religious authorities to "restore their belief and faith." In Penang, religious authorities arrested 20 Muslim individuals for similar offenses.

In corruption investigations, after a senior police official involved in the investigation submits a written application, the law empowers a deputy public prosecutor to authorize interception of any messages sent or received by a suspect. Information obtained in this way is admissible as evidence in a corruption trial. Security forces have broad authority to install surveillance devices surreptitiously on private property. In addition public prosecutors may authorize police to intercept postal and telecommunications messages if a prosecutor judges these likely to contain information regarding a terrorist offense. Intercepted communications from such efforts are admissible in court.

The government bans membership in unregistered political parties and organizations.

The government does not recognize marriages between Muslims and non-Muslims and children born of such marriages are considered illegitimate.

SECTION 2. RESPECT FOR CIVIL LIBERTIES, INCLUDING

a. Freedom of Speech and Press

The constitution provides for freedom of speech and press, although the government restricted freedom of expression and intimidated journalists into practicing self-censorship. Government representatives cited protection of national security, public order, and friendly relations with other countries as reasons for restrictions on the media.

Freedom of Speech: The constitution provides that laws may impose restrictions on freedom of speech "in the interest of the security of the Federation… [or] public order." The election law makes it an offense for a candidate to "promote feelings of ill will, discontent, or hostility." Violators may be disqualified from running for office. The Sedition Act prohibits public comment on issues defined as sensitive, such as racial and religious matters or criticism of the king or ruling sultans. The Sedition Act, Official Secrets Act, Universities and University Colleges Act, Printing Presses and Publications Act, criminal defamation laws, and other laws restricted or intimidated political speech. Nevertheless, individuals and opposition political parties frequently criticized the government publicly or privately and in online media.

On some occasions the government retaliated against those who criticized it. On March 14, prosecutors charged opposition politician Tian Chua under the Sedition Act for remarks he was accused of making that implied the intrusion into eastern Sabah by Filipino militants (the Lahad Datu confrontation) was a government conspiracy to scare people for political gains. In response Chua stated that he was misquoted and had only accused the government of creating a media blackout during the crisis. Chua was charged a second time in May under the same act along with four other activists for calling on the public to take to the street to protest alleged fraud that took place during the May 5 general elections. Their trial dates had not been set by year's end.

NGOs asserted government application of restrictions on expression was selective. They noted that when Ibrahim Ali, a politician with ties to the ruling coalition, called on Muslims to burn Malay-language copies of the Bible in January, no action was taken to charge him with sedition.

Press Freedoms: Parties in the ruling coalition owned or controlled a majority of shares in two of the three major English-language and most Malay daily newspapers. Businesspersons well connected to the government and ruling parties owned the third major English-language newspaper and all four major Chinese-language newspapers. Most radio and television networks were also owned by ruling coalition political parties or businesses linked to them.

The government exerted control over news content, both in print and broadcast media, punished publishers of "malicious news" and banned, restricted, and limited circulation of publications believed to threaten public order, morality, or national security. In December the Home Ministry temporarily suspended the printing permit of *The Heat*, a recently established weekly news magazine. The suspension came after *The Heat* published an article that depicted Prime Minister Najib and his wife, as well as the Prime Minister's Department as extravagantly spending public funds.

There was some harassment of online media, which were also occasionally barred from covering government press conferences.

The popular online news website Malaysiakini was banned from covering major UMNO events, including the supreme council meetings and the annual general meeting. Malaysiakini purported that the banning was a result of its reporting on an UMNO logging scandal in Pahang five years ago. Malaysiakini was also occasionally barred from certain ministerial press conferences, but these have been selective. The news portal won a legal victory in October when the Court of Appeals unanimously dismissed the Home Ministry's appeal against a High Court judgment that Malaysiakini portal operator Mkini Dotcom Sdn Bhd be issued a publication permit. The government did not appeal the decision within 30 days of the High Court judgment and therefore Malaysiakini can again apply to the Home Ministry for a license.

Although the Ministry of Information issues official accreditation cards to the media, police requested media practitioners to submit names of reporters covering an opposition rally in January, ostensibly for their protection. Independent online media criticized the move and alleged the request was meant to deter journalists from reporting on the event.

Authorities barred journalists from the Philippines from entering the state of Sabah during the Lahd Datu crisis and in February detained and interrogated three journalists from al-Jazeera for six hours while they were reporting on the standoff between an armed group from the Philippines and Malaysian security forces. The then defense minister Ahmad Zahid Hamidi stated the government took these measures to prevent misreporting during the crisis.

Violence and Harassment: Journalists were subject to harassment and intimidation due to their reporting.

In July the Sarawak State immigration department detained and subsequently deported Clare Rewcastle Brown, a British citizen who ran a website and radio station critical of the state government of Sarawak.

Censorship or Content Restrictions: The government censored the media, primarily the print and broadcast media. This was done directly and indirectly by controlling news content; making publication of "malicious news" a punishable offense and empowering the home affairs minister to ban or restrict publications believed to threaten public order, morality, or national security; prosecuting bloggers and journalists for their writings; taking little or no action against those who abused journalists; and limiting circulation of some organizations' publications to their members. A permit is required to own a printing press. Printers often were reluctant to print publications critical of the government for fear of reprisal. Such policies, together with antidefamation laws, inhibited independent or investigative journalism and resulted in extensive self-censorship.

According to the government, censorship provisions ensured that the media did not disseminate "distorted news" and were necessary to preserve harmony and promote peaceful coexistence in a multiracial country. Despite these restrictions, publications of opposition parties, social action groups, unions, internet news sites, and other private groups actively covered opposition parties and frequently printed views critical of government policies. The English, Malay, and Chinese press sometimes provided alternative views on sensitive issues, as did online media and bloggers.

The government occasionally censored foreign magazines, foreign newspapers, and foreign-sourced television programming, most often for sexual content.

Radio and television stations were as restricted as the print media and were predominantly supportive of the government. News about the opposition was restricted and slanted. Television stations censored programming in line with government guidelines. The government maintained a list of public personalities including local and foreign performers, politicians, and religious leaders who were seen to convey messages or practices which "would jeopardize the harmony and unity of the country" and were not allowed to appear on television or broadcast on radio.

The government generally restricted remarks or publications including books that it judged might incite racial or religious disharmony. On October 14, the Appeals Court ruled a newspaper of the Roman Catholic Church could not use the word "Allah" in its Malay-language edition, overturning a 2009 High Court verdict. The church subsequently applied to appeal. The case was pending at year's end.

The Printing Presses and Publications Act requires domestic and foreign publishers to apply to the government for a permit and empowers the home affairs minister to ban or restrict publications believed to threaten public order, morality, or national security. Judicial review may be sought for banned books. The ministry reviewed, censored, and confiscated many foreign publications.

The Home Ministry banned two books during the year, compared with five in 2012. In September the High Court overturned a 2012 ban on the Malay language translation of the book *Allah, Liberty and Love*, by Irshad Manji. Despite the ruling, the Federal Territories Islamic Affairs Department did not drop charges against Nik Raina Abdul Aziz, a Borders bookstore manager charged in 2012 for distributing copies of the book six days before announcement of the original ban. Raina was specifically chosen because she was a Muslim who could be charged by the sharia court, while more senior staff members who were not Muslims were ignored by authorities. Sharia court proceedings were underway as of October.

The Home Ministry maintained a list of 1,519 banned titles.

On March 14, the Federal Court rejected the government's appeal to reinstate a 2008 ban on the book *Muslim Women and the Challenges of Islamic Extremism*. The original ban was overturned in 2010.

Libel Laws/National Security: The Defamation Act governs civil defamation disputes and sections of the penal code govern criminal defamation. Criminal defamation is punishable by a maximum of two years in jail, a fine, or both.

On March 12, then deputy inspector general of police Khalid Abu Bakar reportedly threatened those who criticized security forces after questions about the government's response to the incursion in eastern Sabah emerged on social media sites. Khalid told a press conference he issued orders to "hound those who post statements that disparage or demean the actions of our force."

Internet Freedom

As of the second quarter of the year, approximately 17 million persons (67 percent) of the population used the internet. The government for the most part maintained a policy of open and free access to the internet, but authorities monitored the internet for e-mail messages and blog postings deemed threatening to public security or order. The Malaysian Communications and Multimedia Commission (MCMC), formed in November 2001, is empowered to monitor the internet for content deemed offensive.

The government warned internet users to avoid offensive or indecent content and sensitive matters such as religion and race. In July the MCMC called two bloggers in for questioning after the couple posted a photograph deemed offensive to Muslims.

Criminal defamation laws led to some self-censorship by local internet content sources such as bloggers, news providers, and NGO activists.

The Communications and Multimedia Act requires certain internet and other network service providers to obtain a license. Previously the government stated it did not intend to impose controls on internet use but would punish the "misuse" of information technology. The act permits punishment of the owner of a website or blog for allowing content of a racial, religious, or political nature that a court deems offensive.

In November MCMC Monitoring and Enforcement Division head Zulkarnain Yasin stated that the MCMC blocked 2,753 websites from January to October. In July Deputy Communications and Multimedia Minister Jailani Johari stated that the MCMC had blocked 6,640 websites since 2008 for pornography, malicious content, and copyright infringement. As of November, 10 websites were being investigated for questionable content.

An amendment to the Evidence Act that took effect in 2012 establishes a presumption of fact that any registered network services user is the publisher of a publication sent from a computer linked to that network service. It thus places the burden of proof on the user or owner rather than government investigators. NGOs, the Bar Council, and members of the public criticized the amendment, noting that it could inhibit online activity in areas such as social media or blogs, where site administrators might censor their speech due to liability concerns.

In August Facebook stated in its Global Government Requests Report that on seven occasions it rejected requests from the government for information on 197 Facebook users, as the law did not compel it.

During the run up to the May general elections, independent online media, including the Malaysian Insider and Malaysiakini, alleged they were targeted in internet attacks that filtered content and blocked access to their websites. Along with other news sources critical of the ruling coalition, they maintained they were the targets of distributed denial of service attacks. Malaysiakini also alleged that persons using internet service providers who channel traffic through the state- controlled Telekom Malaysia Berhad had difficulty accessing its website.

Academic Freedom and Cultural Events

The government placed some restrictions on academic freedom, particularly the expression of unapproved political views, and enforced restrictions on teachers and students who expressed dissenting views. The government required that all civil servants, university faculty, and students sign a pledge of loyalty to the king and government. Opposition leaders and human rights activists claimed the government used the loyalty pledge to restrain political activity among civil servants, academics, and students.

Although faculty members sometimes were publicly critical of the government, public university academics whose career advancement and funding depended on the government, practiced self-censorship. Self-censorship took place among academics at private institutions as well, spurred by fears the government might revoke the licenses of their institutions. The law also imposed limitations on student associations and on student and faculty political activity.

The government regularly censored films, editing out profanity, kissing, sex, and nudity. Films were also censored based on certain political and religious content. Films in Hebrew, Yiddish, or from Israel were not allowed to be shown in cinemas. Although the government allowed foreign films at local film festivals, sexual content was censored by blocking the screen until the concerned scene was over. Media censorship rules forbid movies and songs that promoted acceptance of gay persons (see section 6).

In October the MCMC banned singer Ke$ha from performing for reasons of religion and culture. Ke$ha and her team reportedly agreed to modify their planned show, including making changes to her song lyrics and wardrobe, to comply with the government's general guidelines for performers. They were not notified of the ban until the day before the event was scheduled. In September Malaysian officials banned the metal band Lamb of God from playing due to their "blasphemous" work.

In January Vishwaroopam, an Indian film in Tamil, was approved for screening by the censorship board but was subsequently prevented from opening in movie theaters by then home minister Hishammuddin Hussein after an Islamic NGO alleged the movie insulted Islam.

Censorship, however, was reportedly selective. A controversial government- funded movie, Tanda Putera, was screened despite objections from the public about its interpretation of race riots that took place in 1969, and for allegedly vilifying minorities in the country.

On September 19, Lena Hendry, from the human rights NGO Pusat KOMAS, was charged under the Film Censorship Act for organizing a private screening in July of the documentary film "No Fire Zone, the Killing Fields of Sri Lanka." She was released on bail and her case was pending at year's end. If found guilty under the charge, she could face a fine of RM5,000 to RM30,000 ($1,529 to $9,174) and a maximum jail term of three years.

b. Freedom of Peaceful Assembly and Association

The constitution provides for freedom of assembly and association but allows restrictions deemed necessary or expedient in the interest of security, public order, or (in the case of association) morality.

Freedom of Assembly

The constitution states that all citizens have "the right to assemble peaceably and without arms"; however, this right was restricted by the Peaceful Assembly Act (PAA) and through the Public Order Ordinance and the Police Act. While the PAA eliminates the need to apply for police permits (although it allows police to place conditions on the time, place, and manner of public assemblies); bans street protests altogether; disallows peaceful assembly by noncitizens and minors (under 15); and restricts where and when assemblies may be held by establishing exclusion zones within 50 yards of designated locations such as places of worship, schools and other facilities. The Bar Council and several NGOs criticized the law. The government selectively enforced the restrictions in the PAA.

Court cases relating to the 2012 Bersih 3.0 rally, a gathering by a coalition of NGOs devoted to electoral reform, were still pending as of October. These included the criminal case against opposition leader Anwar Ibrahim and two other PKR leaders who were charged with violating the PAA by taking part in a "street protest," disobeying a magistrate's court order during the Bersih 3.0 gathering, and involvement in breaching police barricades. The government filed a civil suit in 2012 under the PAA against Bersih cochairperson Ambiga Sreenevasan and nine other steering committee members seeking RM122,000 ($37,308) in damages. The defendants countersued seeking a declaration from the high court that section six of the PAA was unconstitutional and void for violating the right to free expression and assembly. In July the government and the defendants settled the matter out of court, and the terms of settlement were being negotiated at year's end.

In September opposition politician R. Yuneswaran became the first person to be convicted under the PAA. The sessions court of Johor Baru fined Yuneswaran RM6,000 ($1,834) for failing to give 10 days' notice to police before holding a rally against the outcome of the general elections. Yuneswaran denied he organized the event and refused to pay the fine, arguing he had filed notice on behalf of the state chairman of the PKR.

In February the Kuala Lumpur Sessions Court found guilty two of the 16 persons charged with participating in an unlawful Bersih-organized assembly in 2007. The other 14 were acquitted.

The opposition coalition disputed the results of the May 5 general elections and organized a nationwide series of demonstrations also known as the "Black 505" protests. While the gatherings were allowed to take place with little interference from authorities, police subsequently arrested and charged several individuals under the PAA. All were free and awaiting trial.

Freedom of Association

The constitution provides for the right of association; however, the government placed significant restrictions on this right, and certain statutes limit it. Under the Societies Act, only registered organizations of seven or more persons may legally function. The government sometimes refused to register organizations or imposed conditions when allowing a society to register. The government had yet to act by year's end on the 2010 application of the parliamentary opposition parties to register as a coalition. The government banned the Communist Party and its affiliated organizations as a national security threat. The government has the power to revoke the registration of a registered society for violations of the act. The government did not use this power of revocation against political opposition groups.

The amended Universities and University Colleges Act provides that students who hold a political post are prohibited from conducting political party activities on campus, and universities may ban any organization deemed "unsuitable to the interests and well-being of the students or the university." Students also are prohibited from "expressing support or sympathy" for an unlawful society or organization.

Some human rights and civil society organizations had difficulty obtaining government recognition as NGOs; as a result some NGOs registered as companies, which presented legal and bureaucratic obstacles to raising money to support their activities. Some NGOs also reported the government monitored their activities.

On February 28, the Attorney General's Chambers confirmed it had ended its investigation of the human rights NGO, Suara Rakyat Malaysia (SUARAM). In 2012 five government agencies began an investigation into SUARAM for allegedly raising funds while operating as an unregistered society and for alleged violations of the Companies Act. SUARAM responded that it was registered as a company because the minister in charge of the Registrar of Societies had total discretion in registering societies and that SUARAM registered as a company to avoid "discrimination." SUARAM claimed it was under investigation because of international attention it had brought to the country by its involvement in a lawsuit in France alleging illegal payments and corruption in the sale of French Scorpene submarines to the country in 2002. The NGO remained under investigation by the Companies Commission of Malaysia at year's end.

c. Freedom of Religion

See the Department of State's *International Religious Freedom Report* at www.state.gov/j/drl/irf/rpt/.

d. Freedom of Movement, Internally Displaced Persons, Protection of Refugees, and Stateless Persons

The constitution provides for freedom of internal movement, foreign travel, emigration, and repatriation and the government generally respected these rights, although there were some restrictions, particularly with respect to the eastern states of Sabah and Sarawak. The government generally cooperated with the UNHCR, and the UNHCR reported good access to government officials. The government generally did not impede other humanitarian NGOs in providing protection and assistance to internally displaced persons, refugees, returning refugees, asylum seekers, stateless persons, and other persons of concern.

In-country Movement: Consistent with the 1963 agreement that incorporated Sabah and Sarawak into the country, these eastern states controlled immigration into their areas and required citizens from peninsular Malaysia and foreigners to present passports or national identity cards for entry. Opposition politicians were denied entry into Sabah, including PKR Vice President and member of parliament Nurul Izzah in May and PKR Vice President and member of parliament Tian Chua in April. Bersih (also known as the Coalition for Clean and Fair Elections), a consortium of NGOs dedicated to electoral reform, cochairperson Ambiga Sreenevasan, who was denied entry to Sarawak in April 2011 during the state election campaign, remained under a ban on travel to Sarawak. Some opposition politicians and activists were also barred from entering states in East Malaysia, during the national elections. Among them were opposition members of parliament Tian Chua in April and Nurul Izzah in late May.

The government regulated the internal movement of provisionally released ISA detainees.

Foreign Travel: Although the government lifted a freeze on travel to Israel in 2011, citizens must apply for government permission to go there. According to Christian groups, this permission was difficult to obtain. Groups may travel through their churches only and must get permission from the Ministry of Home Affairs. Authorities imposed quotas on the number allowed on each trip (20 people) and the length (seven days). Churches also are required to prove that those going on the trip are members of the church. The government stated that because the country has no formal relations with Israel and there is a volatile security situation, the imposed conditions are fair.

Exile: The constitution provides that no citizen may be banished or excluded from the country. Chin Peng, the former leader of the communist insurgency, resided in Thailand because he was either unable or unwilling to satisfy a court ruling compelling him to show identification papers proving his citizenship. In September he died in exile. Dissident blogger Raja Petra Kamarudin remained in self-imposed exile in London.

Noncitizens were deported under the Immigration Act.

Protection of Refugees

Access to Asylum: The country's laws do not provide for the granting of asylum or refugee status, and the government has not established a system for providing protection to refugees. Despite UNHCR advocacy, the government did not provide legal protection against the expulsion or return of refugees to countries where their lives or freedom would be threatened on account of their race, religion, nationality, membership in a particular social group, or political opinion. At the same time, the government generally cooperated with the UNHCR and occasionally reported potential persons of concern to the UNHCR.

The legal framework for the protection of refugees, however, remains inadequate.

As of October the UNHCR reported 125,375 persons as asylum seekers and refugees, approximately 93 percent of whom were from Burma, with Chin and Rohingya being the most numerous groups, followed by Rakhine (Arakanese), Kachin, Mon, Karen and others. Other sizeable groups of refugees were from Sri Lanka, Somalia, Iraq, Pakistan, Iran, and Afghanistan. The UNHCR noticed an uptick in arrivals from Syria.

According to the UNHCR, other persons of concern included 80,000 Filipinos in the province of Sabah, an estimated 49,000 unregistered asylum seekers, and 40,000 stateless Tamil and members of other indigenous groups.

According to official statistics, in the first quarter of the year, there were 10 landings of boats carrying Rohingya asylum seekers to the country. The Rohingya were detained and had access to the UNHCR within one month.

Refoulement: There were no reports of government deportation of refugees or asylum seekers with UNHCR refugee cards. There were occasional reports by refugees of needing to pay bribes to police to avoid detention, despite carrying a UNHCR card. The UNHCR stated that there have been no confirmed reports of deportation of Burmese refugees at the border since July 2009.

An international NGO reported that in December 2012 the government deported six Muslim-minority Uighurs from detention in the country back to China. The six persons had registered with the UNHCR and were waiting for their claims to be processed when they were deported.

Refugee Abuse: The government sometimes detained asylum seekers, either in police lockups or in IDCs, until the asylum seeker's bona fides was established by the UNHCR. NGOs reported that such detention facilities were overcrowded, unsanitary, and lacked adequate medical facilities (see section 1.c.).

The UNHCR received one report of the death of a refugee candidate in detention during the year, a newly arrived Rohingya who was detained in Sungai Buloh prison. Authorities told the UNHCR he was very weak and had a fever when he arrived. He was taken to the hospital and subsequently passed away.

Employment: Although not legally authorized to work, the government typically did not interfere with registered refugees doing odd jobs. The UNHCR reported there were a few cases, however, in which the government brought charges against employers for hiring them. During the year there were official announcements concerning deliberations about allowing refugees to work and the discussion continued in the media.

Access to Basic Services: The government provided access to health care for refugees, but not asylum seekers, with UNHCR cards at a discounted foreigner's rate; however, the costs generally were beyond the means of the refugees. NGOs ran mobile clinics, but access was limited. Refugees did not have access to the public education system. Access to education for refugees was limited to NGO and ethnic community-run schools and the UNHCR estimated no more than 40 percent of refugee children attended school. A lack of resources and qualified teachers limited opportunities for the majority of school-age children. During the year UNHCR staff members conducted numerous visits to various prisons and IDCs to provide counseling, support, and legal representation for refugees.

Stateless Persons

Citizenship is derived from one's parents. The citizenship of one or both of the parents, whether the parents are legally married, and the ability to produce valid identification and proof of citizenship are the key criteria for being able to pass citizenship to a child. As of September the UNHCR estimated there were 40,000 stateless individuals in peninsular Malaysia alone, in addition to approximately 92,943 refugees and 15,393 asylum seekers. The UNHCR estimated there were more than 10,000 children of the roughly 80,000 Filipino workers in Sabah without birth documentation who are technically stateless.

Foreign women often may qualify for permanent resident (PR) status after five years of marriage to a citizen (10 years for foreign men). After two years of PR status, they are eligible to apply for citizenship. While awaiting PR status, foreign spouses of citizens are usually granted visas that allow them an extended legal stay in the country. A local advocacy group for migrant workers reported that in the last five or six years, these processes improved to include shorter waiting times in the processing of PR petitions and visas. Although nationality laws in the country are not overtly discriminatory because of gender, ethnicity, or religion, some unevenness was evident. Refugees were at a particular disadvantage because they often were unable to provide valid documentation to prove citizenship in their countries of origin.

Women may pass their citizenship to their children born in the country, regardless of whether the child was born in wedlock, but men may pass their citizenship to their children only if the child is born in wedlock. Children born abroad, in wedlock, to a citizen father and a foreign or citizen mother may be registered as citizens. Children born abroad in wedlock to a citizen mother and a foreign father are traditionally considered to have inherited the father's citizenship.

Authorities considered children born out of wedlock to foreign women to have inherited their mother's citizenship. Such births may be registered only upon production of valid proof of citizenship. This creates a risk of statelessness because many foreign women are unable to produce valid proof of citizenship, such as a passport. According to the UNHCR, refugees or asylum seekers often do not have valid proof of citizenship. In these cases the child's citizenship is listed as "unknown" on his or her birth certificate. The UNHCR did not have the number of children affected by this issue but viewed it as a widespread problem. These undocumented children were not able to attend public schools or access other services.

Although the children born in the country of refugee mothers married to Malaysian men are eligible for citizenship, the mother may have trouble registering the marriage and subsequently the child's citizenship because of inability to provide a valid passport or identification document. Some observers indicated that children born to Muslim refugees and asylum seekers often had an easier time obtaining citizenship than non-Muslim refugees and asylum seekers. For refugees in Muslim marriages, a UNHCR document or other documentation may be accepted in lieu of a passport.

A number of local NGOs and SUHAKAM did research, conducted workshops, and ran public awareness campaigns on the problem of stateless children.

Individuals without proof of citizenship were not able to attend school, access government services such as reduced cost healthcare, or own property.

The UNHCR may provide birth registration or other documentation in some cases.

By law anyone entering the country without appropriate documentation is considered illegal and faces mandatory imprisonment for a maximum of five years, a fine not to exceed RM10,000 ($3,058), or both, and mandatory caning not to exceed six strokes.

Section 3. Respect for Political Rights: The Right of Citizens to Change Their Government

The law provides citizens the right to change their government peacefully, and citizens exercised this right through periodic elections based on universal suffrage; however, while votes generally were recorded accurately, there were irregularities that affected the fairness of elections, and this right was abridged. The constitution does not limit the difference in the size of electoral constituencies in each district and each constituency, regardless of size, is represented by one parliamentary seat. The size of electoral districts vary, with rural districts generally smaller in population than urban districts. For example, the rural district of Igan has 18,000 registered voters with one representative, while, the urban district of Kapar had over 144,000 registered voters with one representative. This has the effect of overrepresenting the rural vote, which historically has predominantly supported the ruling coalition.

Elections and Political Participation

Recent Elections: The 2013 national elections marked the second time since 1969 that the opposition denied the ruling BN coalition a two-thirds majority in parliament and thereby blocked the government's ability to amend the constitution at will. Opposition parties won 52 percent of the popular vote, 89 of 222 parliamentary seats, 229 of 505 state assembly seats, and control of three of the 13 state governments. Opposition gains came despite the fact that opposition parties were unable to compete on equal terms with the BN coalition because of unequal access to the mainstream media and the gerrymandering that benefitted the ruling coalition.

The discrepancy in size of electoral constituencies allowed for the ruling coalition to win 60 percent of the seats in parliament with only 48 percent of the popular vote. In contrast, the opposition received 52 percent of the vote but only obtained 40 percent of the seats, due to its stronger performance in population dense urban districts.

The government offered 10 minutes of prerecorded television airtime to political parties from both the ruling coalition and the opposition to present their manifestos. The government-influenced mainstream media, however, limited the amount of time the opposition could otherwise campaign on the air, as well as which parties could advertise in the newspapers. In March the opposition-led Penang state government attempted to buy advertising space in a mainstream newspaper owned by UMNO. Chief Minister (governor equivalent) Lim Guan Eng reported that the state was informed by the newspaper it would not accept advertisements for the opposition.

One of the most contentious aspects of the general elections was the quality of the electoral rolls. NGOs and opposition party leaders alleged the government illegally registered "phantom" voters from other districts to vote in tightly contested races, inflated voter rolls, and registered noncitizens to vote.

Several incidents of violence or harassment were reported in the run-up to the elections. In April an incumbent opposition member of parliament, Nurul Izzah Anwar, alleged a supporter of the BN coalition threatened a member of her campaign team with a machete. In Penang five assailants seriously injured two men while they were hanging opposition party flags and an explosive device was set off at a BN rally in northern Penang state that injured a security guard. Threats of violence also surfaced on the internet.

The Election Commission (EC) accredited several national organizations to observe the elections, including the Institute for Democracy and Economic Affairs (IDEAS), the Centre for Public Policy Studies (CPPS) and Merdeka Center for Opinion Research (Merdeka Center). A joint report released by IDEAS and CPPS on May 8, three days after the general elections, stated that the elections "proceeded smoothly and with minimal major issues." They were critical, however, of media coverage in favor of the ruling coalition and reported misuse of government facilities by the BN and doubts about the EC's impartiality and the integrity of the electoral rolls. Their report concluded the elections were "partially free and not fair." Cambodian and Indonesian observers who were invited by the EC along with 17 other delegates from Association of Southeast Asian Nations (ASEAN) countries noted that they were able to oversee the process without issue.

The government did not allow international NGOs or representatives from non- ASEAN countries to observe the electoral process.

Following the general elections, both the ruling coalition and the opposition filed petitions challenging the outcomes in certain state and parliamentary seat elections. Most cases were dismissed by the judge in the initial phase of the electoral court, some went to trial, but none resulted in overturning election results. NGOs and the Bar Council noted with concern that the monetary amount awarded by the Election Court as costs for election petitions that were rejected on technical grounds, especially against the opposition, was not in line with normal costs. In September Chief Justice Arifin Zakaria stated that parties which were not satisfied with the costs imposed by the Election Courts could appeal to the Federal Court.

A Royal Commission of Inquiry was held to look into an alleged citizenship-for- votes program in the eastern state of Sabah. Civil society organizations maintained that the government naturalized immigrants extralegally in exchange for pledges to vote for the ruling coalition.

Political Parties: Opposition parties were unable to compete on equal terms with the UMNO-led BN coalition, and were subject to restrictions and outside interference. The lack of equal access to the media was a serious problem for the opposition in the national elections. News about the opposition was restricted and reported in a biased fashion. Opposition leaders claimed that the EC was under government control and lacked the independence it needed to be impartial.

The opposition organized a nationwide series of demonstrations to protest alleged electoral fraud. Organizers and speakers at some of these demonstrations were investigated under the PAA or the Sedition Act. In September the Johor secretary for opposition party PKR was convicted under the PAA for organizing a protest against the elections outcome (see section 2.b.).

Parliament rarely amended or rejected government-proposed legislation and did not give legislation proposed by the opposition serious consideration. Parliamentary procedures allow the speaker of parliament to suspend members, establish restrictions on tabling questions, edit written copies of members' speeches before delivery, and severely restrict members' opportunities to question and debate government policies.

Opposition-run state governments in Selangor and Penang attempted re-introduction of local government elections but faced resistance from the federal government, the EC, and the courts. On June 27, however, the Federal Court granted the Penang government leave to file a petition to challenge sections 10 and 15 of the Local Government Act of 1976, which prevents the holding of local government elections.

Participation of Women and Minorities: Women faced no legal limits on participation in government and politics. Only two of 32 cabinet ministers were women, however. Women held 23 of the 222 elected seats in the lower house and 15 of the 60 seats in the appointed senate.

The politically dominant Malay majority held the most powerful government senior leadership positions. Non-Malays filled nine of the 32 ministerial posts and eight of the 26 deputy minister positions.

Section 4. Corruption and Lack of Transparency in Government

The law provides criminal penalties for official corruption; however, enforcement generally focused on relatively small-scale, low-level crime. The media reported numerous cases of alleged official corruption, and there was a broadly held perception of widespread corruption and cronyism within the governing coalition and in government institutions.

Corruption: While the government successfully prosecuted rising numbers of bribe-taking officials and persons paying bribes, observers noted the relatively few senior officials prosecuted (or convicted). Following the general elections, Prime Minister Najib created a new ministerial position in charge of governance and integrity and appointed former Transparency International-Malaysia president Paul Low to the position.

The Malaysian Anti-Corruption Commission (MACC) is responsible for investigating and prosecuting corruption of both private and public bodies. An auditor general has the responsibility, set forth in the constitution and the Audit Act, to audit the accounts of the federal and state governments, government agencies, and other public authorities. The MACC reported that from January to August, 315 people, including 109 civil servants, were arrested under anticorruption laws. There was a perception that the government at times used the MACC, as well as the Official Secrets Act and other statutes, to harass or silence opponents.

There were a limited number of reported prosecutions of officials including police and political figures. In June a High Court judge found the newly appointed Inspector General of Police Khalid Abu Bakar liable for covering up the death of Kugan Ananthan, a suspect in a car theft case. The judgment also ordered the government to pay damages to the victim's family.

On May 30, the Court of Appeal upheld a 2011 decision by the Shah Alam High Court to sentence Mohamed Khir Toyo, a former UMNO chief minister of Selangor, to 12 months in jail for graft and illegally obtaining two plots of land for himself and his wife.

The 2012 Auditor General's Report, released during the year, noted possible fraud and abuse in a range of government programs, including the disappearance of police vehicles and firearms, government procurement at highly inflated prices, and poor management of funds and assets.

Whistleblower Protection: The 2010 Whistleblower Protection Act is designed to protect individuals who disclose information on corrupt practices in both the public and private sectors. The act states that anyone who has evidence of a corrupt practice, act, or fraudulent activity may file a complaint and refer the case to court. The whistleblower would be provided immunity from civil or criminal charges. Whistleblowers who go to the media or report information publicly do not enjoy such protections, however.

In October parliament passed a controversial amendment to Penal Code Section 203A, which provides that "whoever discloses any information or matter which has been obtained by him in the performance of his duties or the exercise of his functions under any written law shall be punished with a fine of not more than one million ringgit, or with imprisonment for a term which may extend to one year, or with both." Critics claimed that the amendment contravened the spirit of the Whistleblower Protection Act 2010 by dissuading civil servants from disclosing corruption. Critics noted that the Official Secrets Act 1972 and the Banking and Financial Institution Acts 1989 allowed for the protection of government secrets and that the amendment was unnecessary.

Financial Disclosure: Cabinet members must declare their assets to the prime minister. Senior civil servants are required to declare their assets to the chief secretary of the government. Junior civil servants must declare their assets to the head of their department. The assets, liabilities, and interests public officials must declare are clearly defined and do not include the assets and incomes of spouses and dependent children. Public officials must declare their assets on an annual basis and not upon entry or exit of their posting. Those who refused or failed to declare their assets faced disciplinary actions and were ineligible for promotion. Information contained in the declarations was not made public.

Public Access to Information: The Official Secrets Act prohibits dissemination of documents, including "Cabinet documents, records of decisions and deliberations including those of Cabinet committees" and any other official document, information, or material that may be classified by a minister in the federal government, a chief minister of a state, or similar public officers. Beyond national security, the act encompasses a broad range of documents and information. Critics accused the government of using the act to prevent dissemination of materials and stifle dissent. Observers contended the Official Secrets Act undercuts protections in the Whistleblower Protection Act.

Members of parliament are allowed to obtain information protected by the Official Secrets Act on an ad hoc basis, some of which was then made available to the public.

The states of Selangor and Penang, both controlled by the federal opposition coalition, are the only states with freedom of information laws that allow public access to certain state documents.

Section 5. Governmental Attitude Regarding International and Nongovernmental Investigation of Alleged Violations of Human Rights

A number of domestic and international human rights groups generally operated without government restriction, investigating and publishing their findings on human rights cases. In some cases government officials were cooperative and responsive to their views.

The government generally allowed NGOs to function independently, met with representatives from some NGOs and responded to some requests of NGOs. In some instances, however, the government also took actions against some NGOs. Lena Hendry from the human rights NGO Pusat KOMAS was charged for screening a movie about human rights violations in Sri Lanka (see section 2.a.). Human rights activist Cynthia Gabriel from the human rights organization SUARAM was called in for questioning in August under the Sedition Act for making allegedly seditious statements during a speech at a fundraising dinner.

In March the Registrar of Societies and the Attorney General's Chambers stopped their investigations into SUARAM for alleged violations of the Societies Act and other purported offenses (see section 2.b.). The NGO remained under investigation by the Companies Commission of Malaysia.

The Sarawak and Sabah state governments prevented some domestic activists from visiting their states. For example, the Sarawak State government banned NGO leaders associated with the Bersih movement from entering Sarawak in connection with Bersih activities inside the state. The Sabah State government also blocked two leaders from the opposition coalition from entering the state (see section 2.d.).

UN and Other International Bodies: The government cooperated with some international organizations, including the UNHCR.

The government, along with civil society, participated in the second Universal Periodic Review of Malaysia in October. After the review was completed, NGOs accused the government of not adequately consulting with civil society during the process and of writing a report that did not sufficiently address human rights concerns in the country.

Government Human Rights Bodies: The official human rights commission SUHAKAM was created by an act of parliament and is headed by a chairman and commissioners appointed by the king on the recommendation of the prime minister. SUHAKAM was generally considered a credible monitor of the human rights situation. SUHAKAM conducted training, undertook investigations, provided reports, and made recommendations to the government. SUHAKAM is not empowered to inquire into allegations relating to ongoing court cases and must cease an inquiry if an allegation under investigation becomes the subject of a court case.

SUHAKAM commissioners traveled throughout the country to educate community leaders, including police officials, on the importance of human rights. Commissioners also made several visits to prisons throughout the country to monitor conditions. As in prior years, SUHAKAM noted the slow government response to its reports that touched on fundamental liberties.

In April SUHAKAM released a report on the actions taken by protesters and police in connection with the 2012 Bersih 3.0 rally. The report found that police used "disproportionate force" during and after the rally and noted that police attempted to limit freedom of information by confiscating media equipment, deleting photographs, and arresting and assaulting journalists. The government did not respond to the report by year's end.

SECTION 6. DISCRIMINATION, SOCIETAL ABUSES, AND TRAFFICKING IN PERSONS

The constitution provides for equal protection under the law and prohibits discrimination against citizens based on race, gender, religion, descent, or place of birth. The law is silent on discrimination based on disabilities and sexual orientation. The constitution also provides for the "special position" of ethnic Malays and the indigenous groups of the eastern states of Sabah and Sarawak (collectively, bumiputra), and discrimination based on this provision persisted. One of the requirements for being considered ethnically Malay is to speak the Malay language.

Women

Rape and Domestic Violence: Rape, including marital rape, is a criminal offense, as are most forms of domestic violence. The penal code states that rape is punishable by a prison term of up to 30 years, caning, and a fine. Marital rape does not have a minimum penalty, but the maximum penalty is five years' imprisonment. There is no minimum jail term for a man convicted of statutory rape of a girl age 15 years or less. The government enforced the law effectively. In 2012 rape victims lodged 2,998 police reports, compared with 3,301 in 2011. In 830 of the reported rape cases, charges were brought against the accused, resulting in 156 convictions. Of the 3,419 cases of domestic violence reported, charges were brought in 1,131 of them, resulting in 526 convictions.

Cultural attitudes and a perceived lack of sympathy from the largely male police force resulted in many victims not reporting rapes. Many government hospitals had crisis centers where victims of rape and domestic abuse could make reports without going to a police station. NGOs and political parties also cooperated to provide counseling for rape victims. Women's groups claimed that courts were inconsistent in punishing rapists.

Although the government, NGOs, and political parties maintained shelters and offered other assistance to battered spouses, activists asserted that support mechanisms for victims of domestic violence remained inadequate. There was a sexual investigations unit at each police headquarters to help victims of sexual crimes and abuse. In addition, police sometimes assign psychologists or counselors to provide emotional support. Women's rights activists claimed that police needed additional training in handling domestic abuse and rape cases.

Some sharia experts urged Muslim women to become more aware of the provisions of sharia that prohibit spousal abuse and provide for divorce on grounds of physical cruelty. Provisions in state sharia laws, however, generally prohibit wives from disobeying the "lawful orders" of their husbands and thus were an obstacle to women pursuing claims against their husbands in sharia courts. Muslim women were able to file complaints in civil courts.

Reports of rape and spousal abuse drew considerable government, NGO, and press attention. Under the Domestic Violence Act, anyone who uses violence against a protected person to willfully contravene a protection order may be punished by imprisonment of up to one year and a maximum fine of RM2,000 ($611). In extreme cases involving "grievous hurt" inflicted using a deadly weapon, the maximum imprisonment increases to 20 years. Women's groups criticized the act as inadequate and called for a broadening of the definition of rape to include husbands forcing themselves on their wives and other forms of sexual assault. They also believed the act failed to protect women in immediate danger because it requires that separate reports of abuse be filed with both the Social Welfare Department and police, causing a delay in the issuance of a restraining order. Cases also required visible evidence of physical injury.

In 2012 an amendment to the Domestic Violence Act that expanded the definition of domestic violence to include mental, emotional, and psychological abuse as well as physical violence took effect. It also allows courts to issue protective orders to prevent third parties from physically abusing, or even communicating with, victims of domestic violence and allows police to arrest a perpetrator when a protective order has been violated. Activists welcomed the amendment but pressured the government to amend it further to cover stalking and intimidation, relationships between unmarried persons, and make domestic violence a separate offense under the penal code.

Women's rights groups most often pointed to the lack of support from police as the main obstacle of enforcing the new law. For example, on June 25, a woman in Penang suffered burns on more than 60 percent of her body after allegedly being set on fire by her husband. Women's groups noted that at least five police reports were made by the victim and her family claiming abuse had taken place repeatedly. The attack occurred four days after the victim was granted an interim protection order, which the women's groups contended was not enforced by police.

Up to 120 police officers participated in four training sessions on the Domestic Violence Act during the year.

Female Genital Mutilation/Cutting (FGM/C): In 2009 the Fatwa Committee of the country's National Council of Islamic Religious Affairs ruled that "female circumcision" was obligatory for Muslims but "if found to be harmful to health must be avoided." In 2012 a university study reported that of more than 1,000 women interviewed, more than 90 percent of Muslim respondents stated that they were circumcised. The most common reasons cited for its practice were religious obligation, hygienic purposes, and cultural tradition. The Ministry of Health responded to the fatwa by developing guidelines for the practice of female circumcision and allowed the practice to take place in health-care facilities, where, prior to the fatwa, it was prohibited. NGOs reported FGM/C was also performed privately outside of government clinics. The practice reportedly gained popularity, even among adult women, converts to Islam, and in urban centers (see Children below).

Sexual Harassment: The law prohibits a person in authority from using his position to intimidate a subordinate into having sexual relations. A government voluntary code of conduct provides a detailed definition of sexual harassment intended to raise public awareness of the problem, but women's groups advocated passage of a separate law on sexual harassment. In past years the Malaysian Employers Federation opposed attempts to legislate against sexual harassment in the workplace, arguing government-imposed policies would unduly restrict the management of labor relations. Some observers noted that authorities took claims seriously, but victims were often reluctant to report sexual harassment because of embarrassment, the difficulty of proving the offense, and trial length.

The Employment (Amendment) Act 2012 makes certain forms of sexual harassment in the workplace criminal offenses. Under the act, sexual harassment encompasses complaints in the employer-employee relationship including sexual harassment complaints made by an employee against another employee, an employee against an employer, or an employer against an employee. It excludes complaints by or against independent contractors. Employers are obligated to inquire into most sexual harassment complaints in a prescribed manner. The penalty for noncompliance is a fine not exceeding RM10, 000 ($3,058).

Advocacy groups, such as the Association of Women Lawyers, stated the provisions pertaining to sexual harassment under the Employment Act were not comprehensive enough to provide help to victims. The association advocated for passage of a separate sexual harassment bill making it compulsory for employers to formulate sexual harassment policies.

Reproductive Rights: Couples and individuals have the right to decide the number, spacing, and timing of their children. Information on family planning was readily available from government and NGO sources. Contraceptives such as birth-control pills and condoms were permitted and were locally available. Estimates of contraceptive use by women remained at approximately 50 percent. Skilled medical personnel attended a large majority of births, and women generally had access to postpartum care.

Discrimination: The constitution prohibits discrimination against citizens based on gender. The law allows polygyny for Muslims, which a small minority of men practiced. Islamic inheritance law generally favors male offspring and relatives. A small but steadily increasing number of women obtained divorces under the provisions of sharia that allow for divorce without the husband's consent. Non- Muslim women are subject to civil and criminal law but not sharia. The constitution gives men and women equal rights to inherit, acquire, own, manage, or dispose of any property, including land. Within the matriarchal Minangkabau community, women are favored in the sense that ownership of hereditary or tribal lands is restricted to women. The Guardianship of Women and Infants Act gives mothers equal parental rights. Four states extend the provisions of the act to Muslim mothers, and women's groups continued to urge the other states to do the same.

The law requires equal pay for men and women workers for work of equal value. NGOs reported, however, continued discrimination against women in the workplace in terms of promotion and salary.

Women experienced some economic discrimination in access to employment. The UN Development Program Country Program report for Malaysia (2013-2015) noted participation in the labor market for women was 46.1 percent compared to 78.7 percent for men.

According to the UN Development Program, women made up 36 percent of the labor force, which it defined as women ages 15 to 64 actively engaging in the labor market, by either working or actively looking for work. In June Prime Minister Najib stated women occupied 33 percent of decision-making positions in the public sector. The law provides that women in the private sector are entitled to 60 days' maternity leave and women in civil service are entitled to 90 days' maternity leave. Men are not entitled to paternity leave. Some pregnant women experienced employment discrimination. Employers routinely asked women their marital status during job interviews.

The government undertook a number of initiatives to promote equality for women and the full and equal participation of women in education and the workforce. The Women's Ministry developed programs and workshops to encourage women to enter the business community and operate small- and medium-sized enterprises. Women outnumber men in universities. A leading public university, Universiti Kebangsaan Malaysia, reported approximately 70 percent female enrollment in its 2012 academic year.

The Women, Family and Community Development Ministry established a Women Directors Registry, which compiled data on qualified women. The ministry also implemented a training program that included coaching on technical and soft skills.

Children

Birth Registration: Citizenship is derived from one's parents (see section 2.d.). By law parents must register a child within 14 days of birth. Authorities require citizens to provide their marriage certificate and both parents' government identity card. Noncitizens must provide a passport or travel documents. Parents applying for late registration must prove the child was born in the country. Authorities do not enter the father's information for a child born out of wedlock unless there is a joint application by the mother and the person claiming to be the father. Authorities do not register children born to illegal immigrants or asylum seekers. The UNHCR registered children born to refugees. Marriages between Muslims and non-Muslims are officially void. Couples in such marriages had difficulty registering births due to the invalidity of the marriage. Children without birth certificates are stateless and denied entry into both public and private schools. Stateless children (like noncitizens) were required to pay higher medical fees, which caused hardship in many cases.

According to the UN Children's Fund (UNICEF) *State of the World's Children 2011*, more than 44,000 undocumented children and adolescents lived in Sabah.

Education: Education is free, compulsory, and universal through primary school (six years). Although primary education is compulsory, there was no enforcement mechanism governing school attendance.

UNICEF's *State of the World's Children 2011* highlighted as a cause for concern secondary school enrollment, which was 71 percent for girls and 65 percent for boys according to 2008-11 data, compared to 96 percent overall enrollment in primary school. The Malaysia Millennium Development Goals Report 2010 also noted 85 percent of students who dropped out of school were from poor families.

Child Abuse: Child abuse took the form of neglect (failure to provide basic needs), physical abuse, sexual abuse, and abandonment of infants. Punishment for child abuse included fines, imprisonment, caning, or a combination these measures.

The government recognized that sexual exploitation of children, including commercial sexual exploitation, and, particularly in rural areas, incest were problems. The law provides for from six to 20 years' imprisonment and caning for individuals convicted of incest. The testimony of children is accepted only if there is corroborating evidence. This posed special problems for molestation cases in which the child victim was the only witness.

According to the Ministry of Women, Family, and Community Development, there were 1,023 reported cases of child abuse, 669 girls and 354 boys, from January to March. In 2012 there were 3,831 cases reported.

In January a magistrate sentenced T. Rajasegaran to 12 month's jail for abusing his three-year-old stepson in September 2012. He was charged in December 2012 under the Child Act of 2001, which carries a maximum imprisonment of 10 years or a fine of up to RM20,000 ($6,116) or both. A video of Rajasegaran beating the toddler with a rice ladle at his house went viral on Facebook.

Forced and Early Marriage: The minimum age of marriage is age 18 for men and age 16 for women and girls. Muslim girls under age 16 may marry with the approval of a sharia court. Although such marriages were uncommon, some statistics pointed to a rise in the incidence of child marriages.

In October mainstream media reported that as of May, the sharia courts approved 446 of 600 applications for marriage involving girls under age 16. According to the Malaysian Syariah Judiciary Department, in 2012, there were 1,165 applications for marriage in which one party, usually the bride, was younger than the legal marrying age. It was also reported that in 2012, 1,022 applications were approved compared with 900 in 2011. According to the 2010 Population and Housing Census, 82,382 girls ages 15 to 19 were married compared with 55,915 in 2000.

There were reports of child marriages, including the marriage of a 12-year-old girl to a 19 year-old man in November. Civil society activists criticized the practice, as well as statements by government officials supporting child marriages as an approved Islamic practice.

In the state of Kedah, the state Islamic Religious Department reported a 35 percent increase in marriage applications involving underage individuals between 2008 and 2010, with 90 percent of them involving girls under age 16. According to a UN report, 7,260 girls between the ages of 10 and 19 underwent premarital HIV screening in 2009.

Harmful Traditional Practices: FGM/C reportedly is common among some Muslim Malay communities, particularly in rural villages. According to the online news portal *The Malaysian Insider*, for many Muslim infants, FGM/C is "a rite of passage whereby a symbolic ritual of pricking their genitalia occurs 40 days after birth" (see Women, FGM/C above).

Sexual Exploitation of Children: Any person convicted of a trafficking in persons offense involving a child for the purposes of sexual exploitation faces punishment by imprisonment of three to 20 years and a fine. Under the penal code, the minimum age for consensual, noncommercial sex is 16 for both boys and girls; however, homosexual acts are illegal regardless of age or consent. Under sharia, sex is forbidden outside of wedlock regardless of age or consent.

The law outlaws pornography but does not address the involvement of children specifically. Child prostitution existed, but children in prostitution often were treated as offenders or undocumented immigrants rather than as victims.

Statutory rape occurred and was prosecuted. Islamic law considers a Muslim girl an adult after her first menstruation, however, which sometimes complicated the prosecution of statutory rape. The victim may in fact be charged with khalwat (close proximity between members of the opposite sex), an offense under sharia, even if she is under the age of 18 and her partner is an adult. A person convicted of statutory rape may receive punishment of imprisonment up to 30 years or caning, or both. According to the Ministry of Women, Family, and Community Development, most victims were under 15 years of age. Sharia courts sometimes were more lenient with males charged with khalwat, although in many cases Muslim men were charged and punished for statutory rape under civil law. According to the Attorney General's Office, as of mid-2012, 859 statutory rape cases were reported (109 involving children under age 12 and 750 cases involving victims between the ages of 13 and 15).

In 2012 the Home Ministry informed parliament that the number of sexual crime and rape cases involving victims under age 16 rose from 1,777 cases in 2010 to 2,419 in 2011.

Displaced Children: The prevalence of street children was a problem in Sabah. Estimates ranged from a few hundred to 15,000 children born in the country to illegal immigrant parents, some of whom were deported. These unaccompanied children lacked citizenship and access to government-provided support and often resorted to menial labor, criminal activities, and prostitution to survive; they were vulnerable to forced labor, including forced begging.

International Child Abductions: The country is not a party to the 1980 Hague Convention on the Civil Aspects of International Child Abduction.

Anti-Semitism

Estimates of the country's Jewish population were between 100 and 200 people. Anti-Semitism was a problem across the political spectrum and attracted wide support among segments of the population. Anti-Semitic books were displayed prominently in many bookshops and other public places. Hitler's "Mein Kampf" and the infamous "Protocols of the Elders of Zion" were on display at the Kuala Lumpur International Airport. Government-owned newspapers and statements by current and former political officeholders, sometimes blamed civil society activity on "Jewish plots" or "Jewish conspiracies."

Trafficking in Persons

See the Department of State's *Trafficking in Persons Report* at www.state.gov/j/tip/.

Persons with Disabilities

Neither the constitution nor other laws explicitly prohibit discrimination based on physical or mental disabilities, but the government promoted public acceptance and integration of persons with disabilities.

The Persons with Disabilities Act of 2008 states that persons with disabilities should be treated equally with access to public services and facilities and that the government and other providers should make improvements to ensure the availability of services. The government, however, did not mandate accessibility to transportation for persons with disabilities, and few older public facilities were adapted for such persons. Recognizing public transportation was not "disabled-friendly," the government maintained its 50 percent reduction of the excise duty on locally made cars and motorcycles adapted for persons with disabilities. The Ministry of Women, Family, and Community and Development was responsible for safeguarding the rights of persons with disabilities.

A public sector regulation reserves 1 percent of all public sector jobs for persons with disabilities. New government buildings were generally outfitted with a full range of facilities for persons with disabilities.

In November disability rights activist Bathmavathi Krishnan was sworn in as the country's second-ever senator with a disability.

A code of practice serves as a guideline for all government agencies, employers, employee associations, employees, and others to place persons with disabilities in private sector jobs. Special education schools existed but were not sufficient to meet the needs of persons with disabilities. Students with disabilities were allowed to attend mainstream schools but accessibility remained a serious problem.

In 2012 SUHAKAM initiated a task force to develop a system to monitor public facilities and policies for persons with disabilities. The SUHAKAM director stated the task force would specifically look into public transport services, facilities in buildings, health care, and education. SUHAKAM also pointed out that the Persons with Disabilities Act of 2008 was not fully enforced; for example, persons with disabilities could not access much of the public transportation system or navigate through cities on the sidewalk. Employers were also reluctant to hire persons with disabilities.

Disability NGOs commented that while the Persons with Disabilities Act contained adequate accommodations, the act was not enforced and therefore was not effective. They lamented that the general public saw persons with disabilities as a burden on society instead of a group of active, contributing members of society, and that this perception was amplified by the way in which they were portrayed by the government as welfare cases.

National/Racial/Ethnic Minorities

The constitution gives ethnic Malays and other indigenous groups, collectively known as "bumiputra," a "special position" in the country, compared to ethnic Chinese or Indians. Government regulations and policy provide for extensive preferential programs designed to boost the economic position of ethnic Malays or bumiputra, who constitute a majority of the population. Such programs limited opportunities for nonbumiputra in higher education and government employment. Many industries were subject to race-based requirements that mandated bumiputra ownership levels and government procurement and licensing policies favor bumiputra-owned businesses. According to the government, these policies were necessary to ensure ethnic harmony and political stability.

Despite the government's stated goal of poverty alleviation, these race-based policies were not subject to upper income limitations and contributed to a widening economic disparity within the bumiputra community. Ethnic Indian citizens, who like ethnic Chinese citizens do not receive such privileges, remained among the country's poorest groups. Another goal of this policy was for bumiputra to hold 30 percent of the nation's wealth. According to several studies, the program reached or exceeded this target, but official government figures placed bumiputra equity at 23 percent. The government did not respond to public requests to make its methodology available.

In August Prime Minister Najib announced over RM3 billion worth ($917 million) of government projects that were offered only to companies owned by ethnic Malays. In September Najib announced an appropriation of almost RM30 billion ($9.2 billion) for the Bumiputera Economic Empowerment program with five initiatives that benefit only the bumiputra, who make up 68 percent of the population. The program includes loans for entrepreneurs, requires every government ministry to hold contracts from large projects to award to bumiputera- owned businesses, and requires state companies to establish targets for bumiputera participation.

In October Home Minister Ahmad Zahid Hamidi was quoted as supporting a police "shoot first" policy when apprehending criminals. In his remarks, Ahmad Zahid claimed that more than 50 percent of the country's gang members were ethnic Indians, and the victims were predominately ethnic Malays. His statements were criticized for disregarding basic human rights and for the discriminatory nature of his comments in regard to ethnic minority groups.

Indigenous People

The constitution provides the same rights to indigenous people (the descendants of the original inhabitants of the peninsular region of the country and the Borneo states, such as the Penan) as to the rest of the population. The government did not, however, effectively protect indigenous persons' civil and political rights. Federal laws pertaining to indigenous people of the peninsular region, known as the Orang Asli, vested considerable authority in the non-Orang Asli minister for rural and regional development to protect, control, and otherwise decide issues concerning this group. As a result indigenous people in peninsular Malaysia had very little ability to participate in decisions that affected them. The special provision under article 153 of the constitution only ensures "the special position of the Malays and natives of any of the States of Sabah and Sarawak" and does not refer specifically to the Orang Asli.

The Orang Asli, who numbered approximately 180,000 (0.86 percent of the population) and who were found throughout the peninsula except in Perlis and Penang, constituted the poorest group in the country. According to the 10th Economic Plan covering the years 2011-15, 50 percent of the 29,990 Orang Asli households lived below the poverty line. Of these, approximately 5,700 households (19 percent) were considered extremely poor. In 2010 a local NGO focused on Orang Asli rights estimated that these numbers underreported poverty because it considered only Orang Asli living in established villages, not those living deep in the rainforest.

A government-sponsored national advisory council existed to monitor the development of Orang Asli, but a local NGO reported that the council did not meet during the year.

Under the Aboriginal People's Act, Orang Asli are permitted to live on designated land not as owners but as at-will tenants, and they did not possess land rights. The law allows the government to seize land of indigenous peoples with the payment of compensation. Observers reported that over the years, the total area of land reserved for Orang Asli decreased, and some land previously set aside as Orang Asli reserve was rezoned for development. Although the Orang Asli were authorized to reside on the land, these rights were often undocumented. This led to confrontations between the Orang Asli and logging companies. While the government continued development in these areas, the Orang Asli struggled for rights to land.

The uncertainty surrounding Orang Asli land ownership made them vulnerable to exploitation. Logging companies encroached on land traditionally held by Orang Asli as well as that of indigenous groups in the Borneo states. Indigenous people in Sabah and Sarawak protested encroachment by state and private logging and plantation companies onto land that they considered theirs under native customary rights.

In October the Kuantan High Court ruled that a group of Orang Asli did not have rights to land beyond what was expressly conferred under the Aboriginal People's Act 1954, resulting in the tribe losing their village, Kampung Mengkapur, which occupied 7,000 acres of land. The Orang Asli filed a lawsuit against the government in 2010 after the Kuantan state government notified them that the land that they were living on would be cleared for a rubber plantation project. The community was not consulted prior to the state government giving approval to carry out the felling activities and claimed the land as customary lands. The Orang Asli indicated that they would appeal the decision.

Laws allowing condemnation and purchase of land do not require more than perfunctory notifications in newspapers, to which indigenous persons may have no access.

The Penan, an indigenous community of Sarawak, used native customary rights to establish land ownership and stewardship. Each group of Penan maintained its own foraging area, which is passed down from one generation to another. Customary native lands were not always well demarcated. Indigenous rights groups alleged Abdul Taib Mahmud, the chief minister of Sarawak, leased Penan and other indigenous groups' customary land to logging companies and land developers in exchange for political favors and money. Local observers claimed logging companies harassed and sometimes threatened vocal Penan leaders and land-rights activists. The Sarawak Penan Association urged the state government to delineate the Penan's native customary land boundaries, revoke timber licenses that overlapped their land, stop issuing provisional leases for plantations, and halt all logging and plantation development activities on their land.

In November police arrested 10 Penan protesters in Murum who staged blockades for several weeks to protest the Sarawak government's plan to relocate them in order to continue the construction of a hydroelectric dam that is flooding villages and has displaced more than 1300 Penan. In December local media reported that the Penan were offered RM23,000 ($7,033) per family to break down the blockade and move quietly to the land designated by the government as their resettlement area. Local activists stated that the resettlement land had been previously used for palm oil production and was uncultivable.

It was reported the Sarawak state government planned to build 12 hydroelectric dams throughout the state, all of which, according to indigenous rights activists, would adversely impact the lives of the indigenous tribes living there. So far one dam has been completed in Bakun, displacing more than 1500 Penan. The next dam planned could displace 20,000 indigenous people.

According to the *State of the World's Minorities and Indigenous People 2012* Report published by Minority Rights Group International, at least

480,000 people in Sarawak (one third of the eligible voters in the state, where 50 percent of the population is indigenous) were not registered to vote, and members of the Penan community alleged that authorities frequently ignored their efforts to obtain identity cards.

In August SUHAKAM released the National Inquiry Report into the Land Rights of Indigenous Peoples in Malaysia. In the report, SUHAKAM outlined its investigations into complaints of human rights violations against the indigenous population regarding land rights. The report concluded indigenous people are "among the most marginalized and disadvantaged groups in Malaysia" and the provisions in the Federal Constitution and domestic laws safeguarding the land of indigenous people have not been followed.

The SUHAKAM report was initially to be submitted to parliament in April, but due to the announcement of elections, and the subsequent dissolution of parliament, the release was deferred and SUHAKAM was not permitted to table the report for debate in parliament, even after the new parliament was in session. Indigenous NGOs and the Bar Council objected to this and encouraged SUHAKAM to submit the report directly to parliament.

Societal Abuses, Discrimination, and Acts of Violence Based on Sexual Orientation and Gender Identity

Section 377 of the penal code states that sodomy and oral sex acts are "carnal intercourse against the order of nature" but was rarely enforced. It was, however, the basis for the case against parliamentary opposition leader Anwar Ibrahim (see section 1.e.). Religious and cultural taboos against same-sex sexual conduct were widespread.

Transgender individuals were often charged under Section 21 of the Minor Offences Act of 1955 for "indecent behavior" and "importuning for immoral purposes" in public. Those convicted of a first offense may be fined up to 25RM ($7.65) and up to 14 days in jail. The sentences for subsequent convictions may be up to RM100 ($30.60) and up to three months in jail. Local advocates contended that those imprisoned served their time in the male prison population and were often mistreated verbally and sexually by police and other inmates.

In 2012 the High Court in Seremban dismissed an application by four Muslim transgender individuals to declare unconstitutional a law that bans men from dressing as women. Each of them was born male but acted and dressed as women. They had previously been arrested or fined by the Negeri

Sembilan Islamic Religious Department for violating the Sharia Criminal Act, a state-level sharia law that prohibits Muslim men from dressing and posing as women. The court ruled that the Federal Constitution's provision on freedom of expression, which bans discrimination based on gender, was not applicable to Muslims who violated the relevant portion of the Sharia Criminal Act. One individual appealed the decision and the case was pending at year's end.

In February seminars on "understanding issues of LGBT" continued and were extended to government officers, including those from the religious department. These parenting seminars against the LGBT "lifestyle" began in 2012 and were endorsed by the Ministry of Education.

In March Asmara Songsang (Abnormal Desire), a controversial play disparaging the LBGT community and sponsored by the Ministry of Information, Communication and Culture, premiered in Kuala Lumpur. The local press quoted the director general of the ministry, Fuad Hassan, as saying, "We will bring the show to public and private higher education institutions in a few states and major cities... that aims to warn young people about the perils of being lesbian, gay, bisexual and transgender." LGBT and human rights activists condemned the play as derogatory and promoting discrimination against LGBT persons. After Kuala Lumpur, the play was performed around the country in schools and universities.

On October 18, the Friday sermon written by JAKIM alleged that complaints of human rights abuses against LGBT persons in the country were not genuine and actually part of a plan by NGOs to push the LGBT agenda to undermine Islam. The sermon was reportedly in response to reports written by NGOs for the Universal Periodic Review of Malaysia.

In July a transgender Thai national was assaulted by a group of youths armed with steel rods and hockey sticks in Kuantan, Pahang. The victim filed a report and police stated they would investigate the incident. The same month, organizers of the banned gay rights festival Seksualiti Merdeka failed for the second time to obtain permission to initiate judicial review against the police to lift the ban on their event first proposed in 2011.

Other Societal Violence or Discrimination

The government's response to HIV/AIDS was generally nondiscriminatory, although stigmatization of AIDS sufferers was common.

SECTION 7. WORKER RIGHTS

a. Freedom of Association and the Right to Collective Bargaining

The law, including related regulations and statutory instruments, allows for limited freedom of association and for some categories of workers to form and join trade unions, subject to a variety of legal and practical restrictions. The law provides for the right to strike and to bargain collectively, but both are severely restricted by regulations and by sector.

Defense or police officials, or public sector workers categorized as "confidential, managerial, and executive," are prohibited from joining a union. Additionally, the act restricts a union to representing workers in a "particular establishment, trade, occupation, or industry or within any similar trades, occupations, or industries." Foreign workers may join a trade union; however, the Immigration Department bars foreign workers from holding trade union offices, as is stipulated in the Trade Union Act. Contract workers may not form a union because they are technically employed in a different industry (for example, staffing) than that in which they are actually working (such as hospitality). They may not join in-house unions or regional/national unions, nor may they benefit from collective agreements.

There are two national labor organizations. The Malaysian Trade Unions Congress (MTUC) is a society of trade unions in both the private and government sectors and is registered under the Societies Act. As such the MTUC does not have collective bargaining or industrial action rights but provides technical support for affiliated members. The Congress of Unions of Employees in the Public and Civil Services is a federation of public employee unions registered under the Trade Union Act.

While the Ministry of Labor prohibits national unions within the country, there are three territorial federations of unions (Peninsula Malaysia, Sabah, and Sarawak) that are allowed to operate. Trade unions were free to associate with these territorial federations, which must register separately as societies under the Societies Act and which exercised many of the responsibilities of national labor unions, although they could not bargain on behalf of local unions. In companies designated as having "pioneer status," including the electronics sector, workers are not permitted to affiliate with territorial union federations. Trade unions are permitted to affiliate with international trade union organizations, subject to the approval of the director general of trade unions (DGTU).

The law prohibits employers from interfering with, restraining, or coercing a worker in the exercise of the right to form trade unions or participation in lawful trade union activities, including in employment contracts. The law prohibits employer retribution against a worker for participating in the lawful activities of a trade union. The law requires reinstatement of workers fired for union activity.

Most private sector workers and, to a lesser extent, public sector workers, have the right to bargain collectively. The law restricts collective bargaining in "pioneer" industries. Some public sector workers had only a consultative role in collective bargaining that allowed them to express opinions on wages and working conditions but not to actually negotiate. The law imposes restrictions on the scope of subjects that may be collectively bargained. The law explicitly states that issues of transfer, promotion, appointments, dismissal, and reinstatement are internal management prerogatives; therefore, excluded from collective bargaining.

The process of collectively bargaining is complex and lengthy. First, the trade union submits a proposal for a collective agreement to the employer and the employer has 14 days in which to reply; if the employer accepts the invitation, collective bargaining must begin within 30 days. If the employer refuses to negotiate or fails to reply, or there is a deadlock in the negotiations, a trade dispute is deemed to exist and the union may notify the DGTU to take conciliation measures. If the parties are still unable to agree, the minister of human resources may refer the dispute to the Industrial Court for binding arbitration.

Although private sector strikes are legal, the right to strike is severely restricted. Strikes are prohibited in a range of industries categorized, according to an overly broad definition, as "essential." The law denies unions and individuals the right to hold strikes protesting lack of recognition of their union. Strikes are illegal with regard to all collective agreement matters, or based on certain issues not covered by collective agreements, such as transfers, layoffs, and dismissals. The process for conducting a legal strike is unwieldy, and strikes or lockouts are prohibited while a dispute is before the Industrial Court. MTUC officials maintained that requirements imposed by authorities were so stringent that it was almost impossible to strike.

The DGTU enforces freedom of association provisions. Charges of discrimination against employees engaged in union organizing activities may be filed with the Ministry of Human Resources or the Industrial Court. In cases of wrongful termination, the law limits worker compensation to a maximum of two years from the time the employee was laid off. Provisions preventing management from taking reprisal actions against workers for union activity, however, were not effectively enforced. A labor group blamed delays of enforcement not on lack of resources or training but on an absence of understanding of the effect of delays on the workers involved and an accompanying lack of urgency.

The Industrial Relations Act requires an employer respond to a union's request for recognition within 21 days of application. If an employer does not respond within 21 days, the union must submit a written appeal to the DGTU within 14 days, which is to then notify the minister of human resources of its findings. If the union fails to submit the appeal within the stipulated period or the minister decides that recognition is not to be accorded, the union is not recognized. Unions also undergo a competency check by the Industrial Relations Department in order to be granted recognition. In the event the employer challenges the decision of the DGTU stating that a union is not competent then the director general of industrial relations performs an additional competency check.

The government interferes to some degree with trade union activity. For example, the DGTU and, in some cases, the minister of human resources may refuse to register or withdraw registration from some unions, without judicial oversight. When registration is refused, withdrawn, or canceled, a trade union is considered an unlawful association. Workers' organizations have no recourse to an independent body in the event that authorities refuse union registration.

The government prevented some trade unions from forming territorial federations. The textile sector is limited to state-based federations of unions in those states that have a textile industry. Trade unions in Sabah and Sarawak may not form a federation with Peninsular Malaysia-based unions, while the unions in East Malaysia can form a federation. According to the MTUC, none of the four regional electronics trade unions approved by the government in 2010 has been recognized by its respective companies. The fact that antiunion discrimination was not enforced and the inability of unions to provide more than limited protection for workers, particularly foreign workers, created a disincentive to unionize. In some instances, companies reportedly harassed leaders of unions seeking recognition. Some trade unions reported that the government detained or restricted the movement of some union members under laws that allow temporary detention without the recipient being charged with a crime and that some workers were not paid or were terminated because of union-related activity. A terminated worker legally ceases to be a member of his trade union. Labor activists complained that the loss of membership upon termination comes at a time when trade union support and assistance is most needed.

The minister of human resources or the director general of industrial relations orders recognition of a union if at least 50 percent of the workers in the relevant establishment are members. Membership of 50 percent is often difficult to achieve because of the numbers of contract workers and workers designated as management or in official roles and who are not eligible for union membership. MTUC officials expressed frustration about delays in the settlement of union recognition disputes. It was common for such applications to be refused or if approved, the decision challenged in court by the employer to delay recognition and consequently unions have gone unrecognized for one to several years.

The Ministry of Human Resources released 2012 statistics regarding trade union formation, showing the ministry recognized 39 new unions while 68 applications were not recognized, withdrawn, or deemed ineligible.

On August 19, the National Union of Transport Equipment and Allied Industries Workers (NUTEAIW) reported that Hicom Automotive Manufacturing Sdn Bhd and Isuzu Hicom Sdn Bhd terminated 18 workers for allegedly creating a perception that "the companies were involved in politics." The union claimed that the workers were fired because they met with an opposition candidate after working hours in their district before the general elections to obtain commitments on worker's rights. The workers met with the Industrial Relations Department and the company agreed to reinstate them. The workers discussed with the company possible compensation for the period during which they were unemployed.

According to the MTUC, the Immigration Department requested that foreign employees sign contracts with conditions including the following: The employee may not marry a citizen or participate in political or trade union activities; change his/her employment during the contract period; or organize, participate, or be involved in any kind of industrial action during the period of employment.

Many employment contracts for foreign workers contained provisions banning the worker from joining a trade union. NGOs alleged that, in the absence of a formal union structure, the "ring leaders" or unofficial spokespersons for groups of foreign workers were singled out by their employers for unfair treatment, such as withholding work. According to the MTUC, foreign workers with these provisions, although not allowed to join unions, are counted as voting against a union in union elections to dilute the number of votes in favor of the establishment of a union.

Companies increasingly turned to contract labor as a way to avoid paying extensive employee benefits, resulting in a class of workers often referred to as "outsourced workers" who legally are not considered employees of the principal or owner of their workplace. The Employment Act of 1955, as amended, legally exempts the labor supplier from certain legal obligations of employers towards employees who are outsourced workers, including with regard to freedom of association and collective bargaining.

In addition to the increasing use of outsourced workers, a growing use of short- term employment contracts also contributed to the declining number of workers involved in trade unions. The short-term nature of contract workers' employment is a disincentive to joining and participating actively in trade unions. Trade unions hold general meetings and elect leaders only once every three years, a period that is longer than many short-term employment contracts. Similarly, observers noted that the government, by classifying contract workers as self-employed, further limited their ability to organize.

There have been no industry-wide strikes since 1962, but several strikes took place during the year as a result of employers who refused to implement the new minimum wage requirement. About 2,600 Vietnamese textile factory workers staged a strike to protest their company's failure to implement the new monthly minimum wage, while 1,000 workers from a furniture plant also went on a brief strike. The government subsequently postponed implementation of the minimum wage to 2014.

b. Prohibition of Forced or Compulsory Labor

The penal code and the 2008 Anti-Trafficking in Persons Act (amended) prohibit forced or compulsory labor. Five agencies, including the Department of Labor, have enforcement powers under the law, but their standard operating procedures did not always result in officers actively searching for indications of forced labor. The penalties for perpetrators of forced labor under the penal code are imprisonment of up to one year and an undisclosed fine. The penalties for exploitation of a trafficked person under the Anti-Trafficking in Persons Act include imprisonment up to 15 years and a fine depending on the nature of the offense.

The national antitrafficking council reported that labor officers received specialized training including with other law enforcement agencies to help increase coordination. The Labor Department relied on evidence of three months' nonpayment of wages in order to initiate an investigation into a potential forced labor case.

A variety of sources reported occurrences of forced labor, or conditions indicative of forced labor, in plantation agriculture, the fishing industry, electronics factories, garment production, construction, restaurants, and domestic households, among adults and possibly children (see section 7.c.).

Labor activists and human rights NGOs reported debt bondage often characterized conditions for foreign workers on some plantations as well as in some factories and other businesses. Labor union representatives described a typical pattern involving recruiting agents who imposed high fees which made foreign workers vulnerable to debt bondage.

Passport confiscation, which was widespread among employers of migrant workers, increased workers' vulnerability to forced labor. Although the law criminalizes possession of someone else's passport "without legal authority," the practice occurred with impunity. NGOs reported that agents or employers in some cases drafted contracts that included a provision for employees to sign over the right to hold their passports to the employer or an agent, and in other cases employers reportedly confiscated employees' passports without contractual authority. This practice effectively made some foreign workers captives of the hiring company. NGOs pointed to examples where affected workers, whose passports were being held by their employer or labor agent, were forced to accept harsh working conditions, lower wages than promised and unexpected wage deductions, and poor housing, all under threat of imprisonment or deportation. A November 7 media report also highlighted passport retention and debt bondage at an electronics factory south of Kuala Lumpur. The report noted that Nepalese workers paid exorbitant fees to employment agents to obtain jobs and once in Malaysia, their passports were taken, which, in addition to leaving them without money, prevented them from returning home.

In August authorities arrested and charged two owners of a foreign worker employment agency in Malaysia, Sim Whye Hong and his sister Sim Yee Sie, with 31 counts of trafficking Indonesian women with the intent of exploiting them through forced labor. In September they pleaded not guilty and were released on bail of RM310,000 ($94,800) each. The court ordered them to surrender their passports and report to the police station once a month. The case was pending at year's end.

Also see the Department of State's *Trafficking in Persons Report* at www.state.gov/j/tip/.

c. Prohibition of Child Labor and Minimum Age for Employment

The law prohibits the employment of children younger than age 14 but permits some exceptions, such as light work in a family enterprise, work in public entertainment, work performed for the government in a school or in training institutions, or work as an approved apprentice. In no case may a child work more than six hours per day, more than six days per week, or at night. Government officials did not deny the existence of child labor in family businesses but maintained that foreign workers had largely replaced child labor and that child labor provisions were vigorously enforced.

NGOs and trade unions reported that child labor was not a significant problem. The National Union of Plantation Workers reported that it was very rare to find children involved in plantation work in peninsula Malaysia. Child labor in urban areas was common in family food businesses, night markets, and small-scale industries. Child labor was also evident among domestic workers, especially Indonesians and Cambodians, because of document fraud (incorrect ages on travel and work documents). One NGO reported that stateless children in Sabah were especially vulnerable to labor exploitation, reportedly in the forms of forced begging and work in service industries, including restaurants.

d. Acceptable Conditions of Work

The national minimum wage provision applies to Malaysian citizens only. The minimum wage policy for the private sector took effect for all companies with six or more employees on January 1 and for smaller companies on July 1. By September 30, approximately 600,000 small and medium enterprises received permission to postpone full implementation of the minimum wage until January 1, 2014. Employers who received deferments were not permitted to impose a levy on foreign workers to offset the cost of accommodation or other allowances. Under the new policy, the minimum wage was established at RM900 ($275) per month on the peninsula, and RM800 ($245) per month in the states of Sabah and Sarawak. The new policy affected 3.2 million workers across the country, including in construction, plantation agriculture, and manufacturing sectors. It does not apply to domestic workers. The minimum wage rates fall below the Ministry of Finance published poverty income levels in Sabah and Sarawak.

In July, the Human Resources Ministry postponed the enforcement of the minimum wage scheme for foreign workers until 2014 for small and medium enterprises and some companies that had suffered losses for the past two to three years. More than 5,000 Nepalese workers in Johor protested the delay. Some groups called for a higher minimum wage, criticized the government for not introducing the new rates immediately for everyone, and found fault with different minimum wages for different parts of the country. The ministry also announced that employers would be allowed to deduct government levies on foreign workers from the minimum wage paid to the workers, resulting in a wave of online complaints and other minor protests.

Working hours may not exceed eight hours per day or 48 hours per workweek of six days. Each workweek must include a 24-hour rest period. The law also sets overtime rates of 1.5 times the base hourly rate for regular overtime, two times the regular hourly rate for work on rest days, and three times the regular hourly rate for work on the 10 mandated public holidays. It mandates public holidays, annual leave, sick leave, and maternity allowances. Limits on overtime vary by sector. The limits apply to foreign workers under the Employment Act.

The Occupational Safety and Health Act covers all sectors of the economy except the maritime sector and the armed forces. The act established a national Occupational Safety and Health Council, composed of workers, employers, and government representatives, to set policy and coordinate occupational safety and health measures. It requires employers to identify risks and take precautions, including providing safety training to workers, and compels companies that have more than 40 workers to establish joint management-employee safety committees. The act requires workers to use safety equipment and cooperate with employers to create a safe, healthy workplace.

The National Wages Consultative Council is responsible for recommending changes to the minimum wage and coverage for various sectors, types of employment, and regions. The Labor Department of the Ministry of Human Resources is responsible for enforcing standards on working conditions and occupational safety and health. No information was available on the number of inspectors. MTUC reports that 12-, 14-, and 18-hour days were not uncharacteristic in the food industry as well as others.

An official at the Ministry of Human Resources reported the Labor Department charged 97 employers with various offenses under the labor law during the year and 80 percent of the offenses were related to salaries, stating that "among the offences were failure to pay salary arrears, compensation, and gratuity that had been ordered by the Labor Court." Additionally, it made 103 charges under the Workmen's Compensation Act against employers who failed to insure their foreign workers or report accidents to the Ministry of Human Resources. The department charged five companies under the Private Employment Agencies Act for operating without a license and issued 461 summonses to various employers, of which 67 percent were for failing to report hiring foreign workers within 14 days of employment. The department issued another 10 percent of the summonses against employers who did not pay salaries within the stipulated period, and since 2010 collected RM1.47 million ($450,000) worth of fines. Penalties for employers who fail to follow the law begin at a fine not more than RM10,000 ($3,058) per employee and can go up to imprisonment of not more than five years.

Employers or employees who violate the Occupational Safety and Health Act are subject to substantial fines of up to RM50,000 ($15,290) or imprisonment for up to two years, or both, although the MTUC complained some employers flouted the rules with impunity.

The Workmen's Compensation Act covers both local and foreign workers but provides no protection for foreign domestic workers. According to the government, the law protects foreign domestic workers with regard to wages and contract termination, but excludes these workers from provisions that would otherwise ensure that they received one rest day per week, an eight-hour workday, and a 48-hour workweek. Bilateral agreements or memoranda of understanding (MOU) between the government and some sending states have limited provisions for rest periods, compensation, and other conditions of employment.

Labor contractors may also be prosecuted for violating the law. The government investigated complaints of abuses, attempted to inform workers of their rights, encouraged workers to come forward with their complaints, and warned employers to end abuses. Nonetheless, NGOs claimed that some legal labor contractors regularly used intimidation tactics and physical abuse to prevent workers who were being exploited from seeking justice. The MTUC reported there were no prosecutions of labor suppliers or contractors.

Workers have the right to take legal action against abusive employers. NGOs reported courts generally sided with employees and ruled that employers must pay all back salary and compensate plaintiffs for injuries; however, long delays in court proceedings and rulings often posed obstacles to foreign workers' access to the system of labor adjudication, particularly if they were illegal aliens.

The law permits migrant workers to bring employment disputes to the Industrial Court. Nevertheless, court policy was not to hear complaints of undocumented migrants. Industrial Court proceedings were time consuming, which may have prevented migrant workers from seeking redress through the court system. Once their work visas expire, migrants require "special passes" to stay in the country in which case they could follow the court case but may not work. The passes are valid for one month and cost RM100 ($31) to renew. Renewal is subject to the discretion of the director general of immigration.

Mechanisms for monitoring workplace conditions were inadequate. Private, for- profit labor agencies, themselves often guilty of abuses, were often responsible for the resolution of abuse cases. A May 2011 MOU with the government of Indonesia called for the creation of a joint task force to monitor the situation of Indonesian domestic workers. It provides for one rest day per week (or compensation) and rules on the repayment of recruitment fees. In July Deputy Prime Minister Muhyiddin Yassin announced an amendment to the MOU that raised the cost of hiring an Indonesian maid from RM4,511 ($1,380) to RM8,000 ($2,446) based on costs incurred in both countries. He also noted that the salary of Indonesian maids would not be bound by the Minimum Wages Act of 2012 but would be based on current market prices and the employer. A 2011 Cambodian government ban on new Cambodian domestic workers going to Malaysia remained in effect.

Foreign migrant laborers, legal and illegal, often worked under difficult conditions, performed hazardous duties, had their pay withheld by employers, and had no meaningful access to legal counsel in cases of contract violations and abuse. Some workers alleged that their employers subjected them to inhuman living conditions, confiscated their travel documents, and physically assaulted them. In May a court sentenced a married couple to 24 years in prison after being found guilty of "culpable homicide not amounting to murder" of a Cambodian national who they employed as a domestic worker. The 24-year-old died from prolonged starvation.

Employers sometimes failed to honor the terms of employment and abused their domestic workers. In February a Filipino NGO documented a range of abuses of Filipino migrant workers in Malaysia. Employers reportedly restricted workers' movement and use of cellular telephones; provided sub-standard food and living conditions; physically and sexually assaulted workers; and harassed and threatened workers, including with deportation. An NGO reported in November authorities rescued at least three Filipino domestic workers in Penang from abusive households and took the victims to the Philippines Embassy for repatriation assistance. One worker reportedly suffered sexual abuse on a regular basis.

Plantation workers generally received production-related payments or daily wages. Under a "safety net" agreement, workers are bound to work for 26 days per month, unless unable to do so due to a natural disaster such as flooding or heavy rain, and are paid a minimum of RM650 ($200). There are three main categories of plantation workers: general field, harvest (constituting the majority), and rubber tappers. Bonus or overtime rates depend on the productivity level. For example, rubber tappers who bring in more than the minimum 24.2 pounds of rubber per day receive extra earnings of up to RM2,000 ($612) for the most productive tappers. The Malaysian Agriculture and Plantation Association must approve such agreements in line with the law.

Based on an MOU between the governments of Malaysia and Bangladesh, Home Minister Ahmad Zahid Hamidi announced that new identity documents with radio frequency identification, biometric technology, and a debit card would be issued to all Bangladeshi workers in Malaysia beginning in 2014. The card would purportedly limit the ability of workers to change jobs and would entail a fine of up to RM12,000 ($367) if they do so. Workers are to be required to pay for the issuance of the card.

Tenaganita recorded more than 1,500 cases of migrant abuse involving undocumented workers and 500 cases of employer violations of immigration law in 2011. For the most part, the workers were deported after serving a jail sentence and the employers were cleared of charges.

In: Malaysia
Editor: Paulina Collins

ISBN: 978-1-63321-227-5

Chapter 3

MALYSIA 2012 INTERNATIONAL RELIGIOUS FREEDOM REPORT*

U.S. Department of State; Bureau of Democracy, Human Rights and Labor

EXECUTIVE SUMMARY

The constitution protects religious freedom with some exceptions. Portions of the constitution, as well as other laws and policies, place some restrictions on religious freedom and in practice the government generally enforced those restrictions. The trend in the government's respect for religious freedom did not change significantly during the year. The constitution gives federal and state governments the power to "control or restrict the propagation of any religious doctrine or belief among persons professing the religion of Islam." The government maintains a dual legal system, under which Sharia courts rule on religious, family, and some criminal issues involving Muslims and secular courts rule on other issues pertaining to both Muslims and the broader population. Government policies promote Sunni Islam above other religions. Other teachings and forms of Islam are illegal, and the government maintains an official but secret list of banned sects of Islam. The constitution defines ethnic Malays as Muslim from birth. Muslims may not legally convert

* This is an edited, reformatted and augmented version of a report released by the U.S. Department of State; Bureau of Democracy, Human Rights and Labor, dated May 2013.

to another religion except in extremely rare circumstances, although members of other religions may convert to Islam. Minority religious groups remained generally free to practice their beliefs.

There were reports of societal abuse and discrimination based on religious affiliation, belief, or practice, including reports of child marriages as an approved practice of Islam. Civil society organizations continued to criticize this practice.

Embassy representatives maintained an active dialogue with the government and with leaders and representatives of various religious groups, including those not officially recognized by the government. The ambassador visited and met with religious leaders across the country to emphasize the importance of religious freedom and tolerance among religions.

SECTION I. RELIGIOUS DEMOGRAPHY

The population is approximately 29.6 million, according to 2010 census data from the Malaysian Department of Statistics. Census figures indicate that 61.3 percent of the population practices Islam; 19.8 percent Buddhism; 9.2 percent Christianity; 6.3 percent Hinduism; and 1.3 percent Confucianism, Taoism, and other traditional Chinese philosophies and religions. Other minority religious groups include animists, Sikhs, and Bahais. Ethnic Malay Muslims account for approximately 55 percent of the population. Several of the most prominent political parties are organized along ethnic and/or religious lines. The majority of Christians reside in the eastern states of Sabah and Sarawak.

SECTION II. STATUS OF GOVERNMENT RESPECT FOR RELIGIOUS FREEDOM

Legal/Policy Framework

Freedom of religion is written into the constitution as a protected right; however, portions of the constitution, as well as other laws and policies, place restrictions on religious freedom. Article 11 states that “every person has the right to profess and practice his religion,” but gives state and federal governments the power to "control or restrict the propagation of any religious doctrine or belief among persons professing the religion of Islam." Article 3 states that "Islam is the religion of the Federation" and "Parliament may by law make provisions for regulating Islamic religious affairs." Article 160 defines ethnic Malays as Muslim from birth. The constitution identifies the traditional rulers, also known as sultans, as the "Heads of Islam" within their respective states. Sultans are present in nine of the country's 13 states; in the remaining four states and the federal territories, the highest Islamic authority is the king. The law allows citizens and organizations to sue the government for constitutional violations of religious freedom. Federal law has constitutional precedence over state law, but the constitution provides that issues of Islamic law are state, rather than federal, matters.

The constitution establishes the power of the federal judiciary by creating two high courts of equal and independent authority, one in Peninsular Malaysia and one in Eastern Malaysia. However, a 1988 constitutional amendment provides that these courts have no jurisdiction in respect to any matter within the jurisdiction of the Sharia courts. This ambiguity regarding Sharia versus secular law remains unresolved. Civil courts generally rule in favor of the government in matters concerning Islam. However, civil courts generally cede authority to Sharia courts in cases concerning conversion from Islam, and Sharia courts remain reluctant to allow such conversions.

The Department of Islamic Development Malaysia (JAKIM) within the prime minister's office establishes federal guidelines concerning what constitutes "deviant" behavior or belief. The government forbids religious assembly and worship for what the government deems as "deviant" sects such as Shia, Ahmadiyyah, and Al-Arqam. Members of banned sects may not speak freely about their religious beliefs. The government may detain Muslims who deviate from accepted Sunni principles and subject them to mandatory "rehabilitation" in centers that teach and enforce government-approved Islamic practices. State-level Sharia courts also have the authority to order individuals who seek to convert from Islam or who profess belief in a "deviant" Islamic sect to enter religious rehabilitation centers. The government forbids individuals to leave such centers until they complete the program, which varies in length, but can often last approximately six months.

The law strictly forbids proselytizing of Muslims by non-Muslims, but allows and supports Muslims proselytizing others. Muslims who wish to convert from Islam face tremendous obstacles because neither the right to leave Islam nor the legal process of conversion is clearly defined in law.

The government places some restrictions on religious assembly and denies legal status to certain religious groups. The Registrar of Societies, under the Home Ministry, determines whether a religious group may be registered and thereby qualify for government grants and other benefits. The registrar has no consistent policy or transparent criteria for determining whether to register religious groups. In cases where the government refuses to register a religious group, the group may pursue registration under the Companies Act. Examples included Jehovah's Witnesses and The Church of Jesus Christ of Latter-day Saints (Mormons). Registration under the Companies Act confers some protection of religious freedom, but precludes government funding.

Officials at the federal and state government levels oversee Islamic religious activities, and sometimes influence the content of sermons, use mosques to convey political messages, limit public expression, and prevent certain imams from speaking at mosques. State governments are legally responsible for the administration of mosques in the thirteen states, including appointing imams and providing guidance on the content of sermons. In the three federal territories, the Federal Territories Islamic Department (JAWI) carries out these responsibilities.

Conflicts and inconsistencies among the constitution, the penal code, and Sharia law continue unresolved. Although federal law exempts women from caning, Sharia law does not. Caning under Malaysian criminal law is carried out with a half-inch-thick wooden cane that could cause welts and scarring; under Sharia law, a smaller cane is used, the subject is fully covered with a robe, and the caning official cannot lift the cane above his shoulder, thus reducing the impact.

Authorities at the state level administer Sharia laws through Islamic courts and have jurisdiction over all Muslims. Sharia laws and the degree of their enforcement vary by state and can be influenced by respective religious departments of the state. State governments impose Sharia law on Muslims in some cultural and social matters, but generally do not interfere with the religious practices of non-Muslim communities; however, debates continue regarding states incorporating elements of Sharia law, such as khalwat (being in close physical proximity with an unrelated member of the opposite sex), into secular civil and criminal law. Although specific punishments for violation of khalwat vary from state to state, it is typically punishable by some combination of imprisonment up to two years, a fine of RM 3,000 ($940), or several strokes of the cane.

Laws and government policies do not restrict the rights of non-Muslims to change their religious beliefs and affiliation. Conversion to Islam, however,

High Court rejected Patmanathan's application and granted Gandhi custody of her children. Patmanathan appealed the decision and retained custody of the youngest child, despite a court order to surrender the child to Gandhi. In July 2010, the High Court allowed Gandhi's application for judicial review to nullify the children's conversion to Islam. The High Court heard the case in September 2011. On November 27, the Federal Court ruled that Patmanathan had failed to present the appropriate papers to appeal the 2010 custody decision by the High Court in a timely manner and had therefore lost the right to appeal. The decision regarding the conversion of the children was still pending at the end of the year.

After the Internal Security Ministry (which later merged with the Home Ministry) banned the use of the word "Allah" by non-Muslims in Malay-language Bibles and other Christian publications in 2008, the Roman Catholic Church filed a lawsuit against the ban. While the case was pending, the Home Ministry renewed the Catholic Church's permit to publish the *Catholic Herald* (published in Malay, Tamil, and English) conditionally, and directed the church to cease publishing its Malay-language section, to restrict sales to Catholic Church property, and to print a disclaimer on the front page saying the paper was meant only for Christians. The *Catholic Herald* continued to publish its Malay-language version using the word "Allah," arguing the Catholic Church had used the word in the country for more than 400 years. In 2009, the High Court of Kuala Lumpur ruled in the church's favor, holding that the government's prohibition on the *Catholic Herald*'s use of the word "Allah" was unconstitutional. The government appealed and in January 2010 the trial court issued a stay pending a review of the Court of Appeals decision. The case remained pending at year's end.

In February the Court of Appeal upheld the 2010 arson conviction of two brothers for setting fire to the Metro Tabernacle church in Kuala Lumpur, and reduced their sentence from five to two years in prison.

In January the appellate court ordered the Penang High Court to hear an application brought by Siti Hasnah Vangarama Abdullah questioning the validity of her conversion to Islam when she was seven years old. Ms. Vangarama stated she was an orphan when a Muslim Welfare Organization officer took her to the State Religious Department to renounce Hinduism and embrace Islam. As a Muslim, Ms. Vangarama was unable to register her marriage to a Hindu man because the law does not permit Muslims and non-Muslims to marry legally unless the spouse converts to Islam. The case was pending at year's end.

The government occasionally suppressed public discussions of controversial religious issues such as religious freedom, apostasy, and conversion of minors. At a November 3 forum on Islam and the state, the vice-president of the opposition People's Justice Party (PKR) stated that any aspect of compulsion, persecution or discrimination on the basis of religion was prohibited. The pro-government mainstream press subsequently criticized her for allegedly condoning apostasy among Muslims.

In 2011, a Shia Muslim sued the Selangor Islamic Department (JAIS) and an official at the newspaper *Utusan Malaysia* for defaming him as a "dangerous person" for his involvement in activities that were the subject of a December 2010 JAIS raid on a Shia group meeting in Gombak, Selangor. During the raid, 128 Shias were arrested, including an Iranian who was giving a sermon, and charged with insulting, questioning, violating, and disobeying a religious decree issued by the state mufti. Two of those arrested also faced charges for unlawful "teaching, 'clarification,' or performance of any rites or actions relating to Islam," as well as "relating, propagating, or spreading views on any issue, teaching or Sharia judgment that goes against fatwas already in force in Selangor." The Sharia and civil court cases remained pending at year's end.

The trial of a Shia religious leader and three Shia group members, arrested by religious authorities and police in 2011, was pending at year's end. The four were arrested at a Shia gathering being held to celebrate the birthday of Fatimah az-Zahra, a daughter of the Prophet Muhammad, and were later released on bail.

Strict enforcement of Sharia law in some states placed additional restrictions on Muslims, who were affected by Sharia court sentences such as caning for violations including alcohol consumption and khalwat. Islamic officials stated that the intent was not to injure, but to make offenders ashamed of their sins so that they would repent and not repeat the offense.

Non-Muslim family members, including spouses and children, continued to lose all rights to inheritances in Sharia court in cases of conversion by one spouse to Islam.

Religious NGOs contended that Sharia courts did not give equal weight to the testimony of women. Several NGOs dedicated to the advancement of women's rights complained that women did not receive fair treatment from Sharia courts, primarily in matters of divorce, child custody, and enforcement of alimony payments.

State Islamic religious enforcement officers continued to have the authority to accompany police on raids of private premises and public establishments, to enforce Sharia law, including violations such as indecent dress, distribution of banned publications, alcohol consumption, or khalwat. On May 23, the Federal Territories Religious Department (JAWI) raided a bookstore in Kuala Lumpur and arrested Muslim employee Nik Raina under Sharia law for distribution of the book, *Allah, Liberty and Love*, a book which had not yet been banned. The Home Ministry reviewed the book on May 29 and banned it on June 14, weeks after the arrest. Reportedly, Ms. Raina was arrested because she was the highest ranking Muslim working in the store at the time. The minister of home affairs declared that JAWI was empowered to arrest Ms. Raina, although there was no prohibition order in place on the day the book was confiscated. Ms. Raina was released within hours. On June 19, she was officially charged in Sharia court. The case was pending at the end of the year.

The Selangor Islamic Affairs Council (MAIS) continued to prohibit all non- Muslims from entering mosques and suraus (a small mosque or prayer room) in Selangor without MAIS permission, as a result of a 2010 controversy that occurred when a non-Muslim female opposition parliamentarian entered a mosque without proper head covering. According to a 2010 National Fatwa Council ruling, non- Muslims could enter mosques as long as they were properly attired and did not violate the sanctity of the mosque.

According to the Malaysian Consultative Council of Buddhists, Christians, Hindus, Sikhs, and Taoists (MCCBCHST), the government continued its practice of restricting visas for foreign Muslim and non-Muslim clergy under the age of 40 as a means of preventing "militant clergy" from entering the country. While representatives of non-Muslim groups did not sit on the immigration committee that approved visa requests, the committee sought MCCBCHST recommendations in most non-Muslim cases.

The government placed or maintained restrictions on some religious customs and sought to enforce certain religious precepts. Observers reported increased quantity and volume of broadcasts from mosques and other Muslim places of worship or learning over public address systems. The government continued to place some restrictions on religious expression, including with respect to religious teaching, use of religious clothing and symbols, proselytism, and religious publishing.

The National Fatwa Council issued a fatwa banning foreign exchange trading by individuals or unregistered moneychangers using an electronic platform, to ensure that financial transactions adhered to Islamic law.

The government continued to require all Muslim civil servants to attend approved religion classes, and several government agencies pressured non-Muslim women to wear headscarves while attending official functions. However, this was not strictly enforced.

The government of Kelantan, considered the country's most religiously conservative state, maintained its ban on Mak Yong, a traditional Malay dance drama performed for 800 years, due to its animist elements, and on Wayang Kulit, a form of shadow puppetry, because of its Hindu influences and its focus on folklore and mythical characters considered un-Islamic. The state also prohibited the sale of lottery tickets and advertisements showing what it considered to be inappropriately dressed women. Kelantan's dress code prohibited Muslim women from wearing clothes exposing more than their faces and hands. The law also stipulated that non-Muslim women should avoid dressing "sexily or indecently." Violators of the dress code faced fines up to RM 500 ($156). Kelantan also enforced headscarf requirements for Muslim women, imposing fines for violations. Kelantan regulations required men and women to form separate lines at supermarkets, although the rule reportedly was not enforced. Kelantan courts also fined couples who sat too closely in public areas, such as on park benches.

In October a public school teacher reportedly slapped four non-Muslim Orang Asli (indigenous) students for not reciting an Islamic prayer. The Education Department, the Orang Asli Development Department (JAKOA) and the teacher involved apologized for the incident; however, one week later the Rural and Regional Development Minister denied the incident. The parents of the students filed a police report and stated that they were unaware that their children, who were attending an exclusively Orang Asli school, were being taught Islamic studies. There was no further action on the case by year's end.

Some indigenous people in Sabah and Sarawak complained of errors in the names printed on their national identity cards, misleading the reader to believe that the card holder was Muslim.

Government representatives or individuals acting on behalf of the government made anti-Semitic statements. JAKIM posted weekly sermons on its website as a guideline for government-employed Muslim clerics during Friday prayers at mosques in the Federal Territories and the states of Sabah, Sarawak, Malacca, and Penang. In March the Federal Territory Islamic Affairs

Department (JAWI) issued an official sermon stating, "Muslims must understand Jews are the main enemy to Muslims." In November a sermon published by JAKIM discussed the "despicable nature" of the Jewish race and stated that "Israel is a nation of ruthless criminals."

Improvements and Positive Developments in Respect for Religious Freedom

On February 21, Deputy Prime Minister Muhyiddin Yassin participated in World Interfaith Harmony Week. Activities held during the week included community activities and religious forums.

On December 26, church leaders announced the government had rescinded quotas, age limits and other travel restrictions previously imposed on Christian Malaysians who wished to make a pilgrimage to Jerusalem.

On November 3, the Perlis Al Islah Association in collaboration with the Islamic Council of Perlis, a government entity, and the Perlis Malay Customs Council (an NGO) organized an interfaith forum "Gateway to Interfaith Goodwill (Gema) 2012." The crown prince of Perlis chaired the forum, which was designed as a platform for interaction among different religions with the hope of creating a better understanding between them. Seventeen religious groups, including representatives of Islam, Christianity, Buddhism, Hinduism, Sikhism, and Taoism, attended the forum.

In a statement to Christian leaders in January, the prime minister promised full consultation when assigning mission school heads. He also agreed to after-school Bible classes, as well as implementation of a regulation that allowed non-Muslim places of worship to apply for tax exempt status for donations received from individuals. This was the first time the prime minister had addressed these issues in a public statement. The tax regulation went into effect shortly thereafter.

Section III. Status of Societal Respect for Religious Freedom

There were reports of societal abuses or discrimination based on religious affiliation, belief, or practice.

Religious converts, particularly those converting from Islam, sometimes faced severe stigmatization. In many cases converts concealed their newly adopted beliefs and practices from their former coreligionists, including friends and relatives. Women and girls faced social pressure to wear the tudung.

There were reports of child marriages, including the marriage of a 12 year-old girl to a 19 year-old man in November. The legal age of marriage is 16 for Muslim girls and 18 for Muslim males, although they may marry before those ages with the permission of their parents and the Sharia courts. Civil society activists continued to criticize the practice, as well as statements by government officials supporting child marriages as an approved Islamic practice.

A vigorous public discussion of the use of the word "Allah" by non-Muslims continued throughout the year.

In September while criticizing an Israeli court decision declaring the state blameless in the death of American activist Rachel Corrie, former Prime Minister Mahathir wrote in his blog, "I am glad to be labeled anti-Semitic. How can I be otherwise, when the Jews who so often talk of the horrors they suffered during the Holocaust show the same Nazi cruelty and hard-heartedness towards not just their enemies but even towards their allies should any try to stop the senseless killing of their Palestinian enemies." Mahathir served as prime minister for 22 years and remained an influential figure.

Section IV. U.S. Government Policy

Embassy representatives maintained an active dialogue on religious freedom with government officials and leaders and representatives of religious groups, including those not officially recognized by the government. The ambassador met with royal rulers at different times during the year and, in those conversations, underscored the importance of tolerance and mutual understanding. The ambassador hosted a roundtable conversation with leaders of Muslim NGOs to discuss religious tolerance. In September the ambassador visited the Sarawak Islamic Information Center to highlight U.S. support for the center's efforts to promote mutual understanding and respect among members of religious groups. Embassy programs also included lecture tours around Malaysia by American Muslim community leaders and imams, roundtables with think tanks and religious and civil society leaders to promote interfaith dialogue, and television and other media interviews highlighting religious tolerance. The embassy arranged visits to the United States for Islamic educators and hosted several iftar dinners during Ramadan. The U.S. government also funded civil society grants and exchange grants for representatives of NGOs working to promote religious tolerance, respect for diversity, human rights, and openness.

In: Malaysia
Editor: Paulina Collins
ISBN: 978-1-63321-227-5

Chapter 4

2013 INVESTMENT CLIMATE STATEMENT: MALAYSIA*

Bureau of Economic and Business Affairs

OVERVIEW

The Government of Malaysia in general strongly encourages foreign direct investment (FDI), although it maintains restrictions or limits on investment in some sectors. It actively reaches out to targeted industries and negotiates incentive packages to attract FDI. Malaysia provides a number of incentives, particularly in export-oriented high-tech industries and "back office" service operations. A wide range of U.S. companies have extensive operations in Malaysia.

Prime Minister Najib Razak (Najib) has made generating new domestic and foreign investment a centerpiece of his economic reform program introduced in March 2010 as the New Economic Model (NEM). Although FDI inflow continues to recover from the effects of the 2008-2009 global financial crises, Malaysia's performance in attracting FDI relative to both earlier decades and the rest of the Association of Southeast Asian Nations (ASEAN) has slowed. According to a recent Organization for Economic Cooperation and Development (OECD) Investment Policy Review of Malaysia, FDI to Malaysia began to decline in 1992, and private investment overall started to

* This is an edited, reformatted and augmented version of the Bureau of Economic and Business Affairs, dated March 2013.

slide in 1997 following the Asian financial crises. Today, FDI levels are at record high levels in absolute terms, but at an all-time low as a percentage of GDP. Moreover, Malaysia's percentage of overall investment in the ASEAN member states is now lower than its share of the group's GDP. The National Economic Advisory Council (NEAC), a blue ribbon panel of experts on Malaysia's economy, in 2010 issued two reports identifying shortcomings in Malaysia's investment climate and proposing policies necessary to improve Malaysia's competitiveness as a foreign investment destination and meet the country's goal of becoming a high-income economy by 2020. Since then, the Najib administration has progressively introduced a series of initiatives to implement the NEM. One initiative, the Economic Transformation Program (ETP), is focused on investment in 12 key economic areas to accelerate economic growth; and a set of policy measures to improve competitiveness. Another initiative, the Government Transformation Program (GTP) addresses governance and quality of life issues, and aims to reduce corruption and crime, to improve education, urban public transport and rural basic infrastructure, and to reduce the number of low-income households. The Tenth Malaysia Plan (10MP) underpins these programs and guides public sector capital expenditures.

Inflows of actual FDI to Malaysia in 2011 increased to US$10.9 billion, up 12.3% from $9.7 billion in 2010 according to the UN Conference on Trade and Development (UNCTAD). According to the Malaysian Investment Development Authority (MIDA), the total value of foreign manufacturing projects approved in 2011 was US$10.77 billion. The 2011 manufacturing FDI approvals were 13.36% higher than US$9.5 billion in 2010. The U.S., Japan, and Hong Kong are the top three countries investing in Malaysia. Up to September 2012, MIDA had approved foreign manufacturing projects worth US$5.25 billion, with Saudi Arabia the largest source of new approved investments.

(Note: Approval statistics are not directly comparable to actual FDI statistics and can be found at www.mida.gov.my. Also, manufacturing investment statistics do not capture investments in non-manufacturing-related services or upstream oil and gas production.)

U.S. FDI in Malaysia is led by the manufacturing, oil and gas, financial services, and consumer products sectors. The total stock of U.S. manufacturing FDI in Malaysia was approximately $20 billion in 2011 as compared to $15 billion in 2010 according to MIDA. Including FDI in the financial and oil and gas sectors, would make total U.S. FDI significantly higher (perhaps more than $30 billion).

From 2009 to 2011, the electronics sector received the largest share of overall FDI. The oil and gas sector became the largest source of new U.S. FDI in 2011 and is expected to remain a focus. For the past three years, manufacturing FDI commitments have centered on projects in the Malaysian states of Sarawak, Selangor, Johor, and Penang – with manufacturing investment in Johor increasing the fastest due to the Iskandar Development Region near Singapore.

As a destination for FDI, Malaysia's attractiveness for lower-wage manufacturing has diminished as years of steady economic growth have increased average wage levels making Malaysia an upper middle-income country. The NEM seeks to move the economy further "up the value chain" to high income status by promoting investment in higher value added manufacturing and service sectors. The ETP identified 12 specific sectors in which the Malaysian government is encouraging foreign and domestic investment, including: electrical & electronics; medical devices; green energy, machinery & equipment; oil and gas, and transportation equipment. Also targeted for growth are a number of resource-based industries and some services sub-sectors including logistics, although the sectors are subject to foreign investment conditions or restrictions.

Through the course of 2011, Prime Minister Najib announced, as a part of the ETP, 113 total new commitments to invest in Malaysia from both foreign and domestic investors with a total value of $57 billion. These investments spanned all 12 ETP target sectors. In 2012, the number of new projects and investment for ETP was smaller with a total of 48 projects and US$17.4 billion recorded. This slow pace is expected to continue in 2013, and in part reflects the fact that much of the investments in 2011-2012 were projects that had been pending government fiscal or policy changes for some time.

OPENNESS TO FOREIGN INVESTMENT

Malaysia has one of the world's most trade-dependent economies with trade reaching 200% of annual GDP. The Malaysian government values foreign investment as a powerful force for the continued economic development of the country, but is hampered by restrictions in some sectors and an at times burdensome regulatory regime. However, the government continues to liberalize and in some cases remove investment restrictions.

In 2009, Malaysia removed its former Foreign Investment Committee (FIC) investment guidelines, enabling transactions for acquisitions of interests, mergers, and takeovers of local companies by domestic or foreign parties without FIC approval. While the FIC itself still exists, it now only reviews the purchase by foreigners of commercial properties valued greater than at RM20 million (approximately US$6.5 million) from Bumiputras (ethnic Malays and other indigenous ethnicities in Malaysia).

The Ministerial Functions Act grants relevant ministries broad discretionary powers over the approval of specific investment projects. Investors in industries targeted by the Malaysian government often can negotiate favorable terms with ministries regulating the specific industry or other regulatory bodies. This can include assistance in navigating a complex web of regulations and policies, some of which can be waived on a case-by-case basis. Foreign investors in non-targeted industries tend to receive less government assistance in obtaining the necessary approvals from the various regulatory bodies and therefore can face greater bureaucratic obstacles.

In 2009 the government announced a limited set of liberalization measures covering 27 service subsectors. In 2011, the government announced plans to liberalize an additional 17 services subsectors during 2012. So far, the government has liberalized 15 of these subsectors, allowing 100 % foreign equity participation in private hospital services, medical specialist clinics, department and specialty stores, telecommunications Application Service Providers (ASP), incineration services, accounting and taxation services, courier services, private universities, vocational schools, dental specialist services, skills training centers, international schools, and vocational schools for special needs. The Malaysian government added an 18th sub-sector of quantity surveyors services. Of the remaining subsectors, liberalizing architectural services, quantity surveying services and engineering services requires new legislation. Legislation that permits the opening of legal services was passed in 2012, but awaits the completion of implementing regulations.

Regulatory Burden

In the World Bank's global *Doing Business 2013* report, Malaysia moved up from 18th to 14th place overall among the 183 economies covered in the survey. Malaysia's most improved rankings were in the standardized indicators "enforcing contracts, resolving insolvency and starting a business". Malaysia was up from 111st to 50th place for "starting a business." Malaysia's worst rankings are in "dealing with construction permits" at 113th, "paying taxes" at 41st, down two places from 2011, and "trading across borders" at 29th place, down one spot. Malaysia made tax compliance easier by improving electronic systems and the availability of software, although it also reintroduced a capital gains tax on real estate. Starting a business was made easier by merging company, tax and social security and employment fund registration at the one-stop shop and providing same-day registration.

Measure	Year	Index/Ranking
TI Corruption Index	2012	54/176 (4.9 score)
Heritage Economic Freedom	2012	53 (66.4)
World Bank Doing Business	2013	14/183

To improve the business climate in Malaysia, the Malaysian government established the PEMUDAH task force, consisting of 23 top-level government officials and private sector representatives with a mandate to identify and evaluate bureaucratic impediments to conducting business in Malaysia and to make recommendations to the Prime Minister on how to address them. PEMUDAH's focus is specifically on administrative reforms designed to enhance the efficiency of the government bureaucracy's interaction with the private sector, not on deeper reform issues needed to address policy-level structural inefficiencies in Malaysia's economy. More information about the task force is available at www.pemudah.gov.my.

Ethnic Preferences

According to many analysts, Malaysia's complex network of preferences to promote the acquisition of economic assets by the ethnic Malay majority and other indigenous groups (collectively known as "Bumiputra") represents a key impediment to the country's ability to reach its goal of achieving high-income status by 2020. Many of the preference policies are opaque, with details of implementation largely left to the various ministries and civil servants within those ministries. Policies and practices vary greatly. Some practices are explicit and contained in law or regulation while others are informal, leaving much ambiguity for potential investors. The civil service itself is overwhelmingly ethnic-Malay in composition. The NEM proposes reforming ethnic preferences in business ownership and social safety net programs, moving to an income based approach rather than one that is ethnicity based. Some conservative Bumiputra groups have voiced strong opposition to any significant changes to the extensive preferences.

In the early 1970s, the Malaysian government set a target of 30% of the nation's wealth to be held by ethnic-Malay Bumiputra. Several studies have concluded that the 30% equity target has been reached or exceeded; however, the topic has proven to be extremely sensitive politically and official government figures place Bumiputra equity at 23%. The government's methodology has been criticized as not fully transparent, and there has been considerable debate over how to account for the value of state-owned enterprises and other government-linked companies or how to measure equity (par value versus market value). The government states that the NEM is returning the focus of preference policies to poverty reduction goals, as originally intended when preferences were established in the early 1970s.

Prior to 2009, all companies seeking a public listing on the Bursa Malaysia (formerly Kuala Lumpur Stock Exchange) were required to reserve at least 30% of its initial public offering (IPO) for purchase by Bumiputra. In 2009, the government eliminated Bumiputra ownership requirements for new listings of domestic or foreign corporations whose operations are mainly foreign based. At the same time, the government also reduced Bumiputra ownership requirements for new listings of domestic or foreign corporations whose operations are mainly in Malaysia from 30% to 12.5%. However, Bumiputra equity remains a consideration when companies apply for an array of required permits and licenses, many of which must be renewed either annually or biennially. Government procurement (and that by most state owned enterprises) continues to be subject to Bumiputra preferences.

Manufacturing

MIDA screens all proposals for manufacturing and related projects in Malaysia, both foreign and domestic, to determine the extent to which they contribute to the government's goals and objectives. These goals are outlined in the Third Industrial Master Plan (2006-2020), the various regional initiatives (Iskandar Development Region and the Northern, Eastern, Sabah and Sarawak Economic Regions) as well as the ETP and the Tenth Malaysia Plan.

Project approval depends on many other factors as well. MIDA may consider the size of an investment, the share of production exported, the type of financing required (both local and offshore), the capital/labor ratio, the potential for technology transfer into the local economy, the ability of existing and planned infrastructure to support the effort, and the existence of a local or foreign market for the output. If both local and foreign firms propose similar projects, the local firm will be given preference. However, all requests are handled on a case-by-case basis. MIDA now has the authority to issue or renew licenses for all manufacturing companies, eliminating a second layer of approval from its parent ministry, the Ministry of International Trade and Industry (MITI). MIDA established an on-site immigration unit in 2007 which has helped expedite the processing of expatriate work visas, as has TalentCorp, a separate recently established agency. Applications for investment in sectors other than manufacturing are handled by the relevant ministries and sometimes require multiple approvals.

Investment regulations are specified in the Promotion of Investments Act of 1986 (PIA) and the Industrial Coordination Act of 1975. The PIA does not address services investment. Private entities, both foreign and domestic, may acquire, merge with, and take over business enterprises. The Malaysia Competition Commission (MyCC) implements and enforces the provisions of the Competition Act 2010, and issues guidelines in relation to the implementation and enforcement of the competition laws.

Distribution Services, Including Direct Selling and Retail Trade

Malaysia began allowing 100% foreign ownership of department and specialty stores in 2012. However, foreign owned larger retailers ("hypermarkets") and locally incorporated direct selling companies must still have 30% Bumiputra equity. Malaysian government guidelines define a "hypermarket" as a standalone self-service store with a sales floor area of 5,000 square meters or more and selling a very wide variety of food and non-food consumer products. The guidelines also include requirements that department stores, supermarkets, and hypermarkets must reserve at least 30 % of shelf space in their premises for goods and products manufactured by Bumiputra-owned small and medium size industries. These guidelines are currently under review by the Malaysian government. The Malaysian government also issues "recommendations" for local content targets, which are in effect mandatory. Domestic companies that seek direct selling licenses require paid-in capital of RM1.5 million (approximately US$397,000), while companies with foreign shareholders must have paid-in capital of RM5 million (approximately US$1.3 million).

Legal Services

Malaysia amended its Legal Professions Act in July 2012. The amendments in principle will allow foreign law firms to practice in Malaysia through a partnership or qualified foreign law firm license and empower local firms to employ foreign lawyers subject to certain conditions. However, a provision reportedly modeled after Singapore's law prohibits practicing litigation except on an ad hoc basis, and restricts work in real property law. While foreign lawyers will be allowed to structure transactions, only Malaysian lawyers will be able to make actual filings. The Attorney General's Chambers is working with the Malaysian Bar Council in developing rules for the amended law, but has not indicated when the new law will come into force.

Until the new law is implemented, foreign lawyers may not practice Malaysian law, nor may they affiliate with local firms or use the name of an international firm. Foreign law firms may not operate in Malaysia except as minority partners with local law firms and their stake in any partnership is limited to 30 %. The Attorney General of Malaysia has authority to grant limited exceptions on a case-by-case basis under the law restricting the practice of Malaysian law to Malaysian citizens or permanent residents who have apprenticed with a Malaysian lawyer, are competent in *Bahasa* Malaysia (the official language), and have a local law degree or are accredited British Barristers at Law, provided the applicant has seven years of legal experience. Malaysian law does not presently allow for foreign legal consultancy except on a limited basis in the Labuan International Business and Financial Center. Foreign lawyers can, however, appear in arbitral proceedings before the Kuala Lumpur Regional Arbitration Center.

Architectural Services

Architectural Services are among the 17 services sub-sectors the Malaysian government pledged to liberalize in 2012. The necessary legislation to allow 100 % foreign equity in architectural firms has yet to be tabled in Parliament, but now is expected to be completed in 2013. At present, a foreign architectural firm may operate in Malaysia only as a joint venture participant in a specific project with the approval of the Board of Architects. Malaysian architectural firms may not have foreign architectural firms as registered partners. Foreign architects may not be licensed in Malaysia, but are allowed to be managers, shareholders, or employees of Malaysian firms. Even after the sector is opened, foreign architectural firms will have to register locally as professional architects similar to Malaysian firms.

Engineering Services

The engineering sector was scheduled to be liberalized in 2012, but pending amendments to relevant Acts have not been completed. Until then, foreign engineers may be licensed by the Board of Engineers only for specific projects and must be sponsored by the Malaysian company carrying out the project. In general, a foreign engineer must be registered as a professional engineer in his or her home country, have a minimum of 10 years experience, and have a physical presence in Malaysia of at least 180 days in one calendar year. To obtain temporary licensing for a foreign engineer, a Malaysian company often must demonstrate to the Board that they cannot find a Malaysian engineer for the job. Foreign engineers are not allowed to operate independently of Malaysian partners or serve as directors or shareholders of an engineering consulting company. A foreign engineering firm may establish a non-temporary commercial presence if all directors and shareholders are Malaysian. Foreign engineering companies may collaborate with a Malaysian firm but only the Malaysian company may submit the plans for domestic approval.

Accounting and Taxation Services

Beginning in January 2012, foreign accountants and auditors have been allowed to wholly-own a practice in Malaysia. All accountants seeking to provide auditing and taxation services in Malaysia must register with the Malaysian Institute of Accountants (MIA) before they may apply for a license from the Ministry of Finance.

Oil and Gas

Under the terms of the Petroleum Development Act of 1974, the upstream oil and gas industry is controlled by Petroleum Nasional Berhad (PETRONAS), a wholly state-owned company and the sole entity with legal title to Malaysian crude oil and gas deposits. Foreign investment takes the form of production sharing contracts (PSCs). Foreign operators include ExxonMobil, ConocoPhillips, Hess, Newfield, and Murphy Oil from the United States, as well as Royal Dutch Shell, and other foreign firms. PETRONAS requires that its PSC partners contract with Malaysian firms for many tenders. Non-Malaysian firms are permitted to participate in oil services either in partnership with local firms and are restricted to a 49% equity stake if the foreign party is the principal shareholder. Terms of upstream projects with foreign participation are determined on a case-by-case basis by PETRONAS.

Electricity Generation and Distribution

Foreign investors are allowed to own up to 49% of an Independent Power Producer (IPP) or power plant in Malaysia. Tenaga Nasional Berhad (TNB) is a state-owned electricity utility company that has a monopoly on electricity distribution in Malaysia. TNB generates its own electricity and purchases electricity from IPPs with power generation plants located in Malaysia. Peninsular Malaysia is connected to an electricity grid with Singapore and Thailand.

Telecommunications

Malaysia began allowing 100% foreign equity participation in Applications Service Providers (ASP) in April 2012. However, for Network Facilities Providers (NFP) and Network Service Provider (NSP) licenses, currently only 70% foreign participation is permitted. In certain instances, Malaysia has allowed greater equity participation, but the manner in which such exceptions are administered is nontransparent. The maximum aggregate foreign ownership allowed in Telekom Malaysia is 30% or 5% for individual investors. Malaysia made limited GATS commitments on most basic telecommunications services and partially adopted the WTO reference paper on regulatory commitments.

Broadcasting and Audio-Visual

The Malaysian government maintains broadcast content quotas on both radio and television programming. At least 80% of television programming is required to originate from local production companies owned by Bumiputras and 60% of radio programming must be of local origin. Foreign investment in terrestrial broadcast networks is prohibited and is limited to a 20% equity share in cable and satellite operations. As a condition for obtaining a license to operate, video rental establishments are required to have 30% local content in their inventories.

Advertising

Advertising falls under the purview of multiple ministries and agencies, complicating the adoption of a single set of advertising regulations and enforcement procedures for all stakeholders in this process. International firms have concerns about the lack of clear and consistent advertising content guidelines, and how some advertisers misrepresent their products and services through advertising. The Government of Malaysia has an informal and vague guideline that commercials cannot "promote a foreign lifestyle."

Foreign content in commercials in Malaysia is limited to 20%. The Malaysian government relaxed enforcement of regulations governing the appearance of foreign actors in commercials shown in Malaysia in 2007.

Financial Services

Banking

The Malaysian Parliament passed legislation in 2012 to update the regulatory framework for the financial services industry. The legislation implements a new 10-year Financial Sector Blueprint that envisages further opening of the financial sector to foreign banks but does not contain specific market-opening commitments or timelines. The new Blueprint, which follows the previous 10-year Financial Services Masterplan, does not significantly break with the existing case by case approach of the central bank, Bank Negara Malaysia (BNM), towards granting foreign banks access to Malaysia. Under the new Financial Services Act, issuance of new licenses will be guided by prudential criteria and the "best interests of Malaysia". Prudential criteria include consideration of the financial strength, business record, experience, character and integrity of the foreign investor, soundness and feasibility of the business plan for the institution in Malaysia, transparency and complexity of the group structure, and the extent of supervision of the foreign investor in its home country. In determining the "best interests of Malaysia", BNM will consider the contribution of the investment in promoting new high value-added economic activities, addressing demand for financial services where there are gaps, enhancing trade and investment linkages, and providing high-skilled employment opportunities. BNM has also stated that it wants to ensure that local banks have at least 50 % of total banking assets in Malaysia (the share at present is significantly beyond that).

In 2009, the Malaysian government announced a liberalization package for the conventional and Islamic financial sectors, but equity limits continue to broadly apply in many areas. BNM sets controls on both foreign and local financial products. Interest rates on consumer savings accounts and fixed deposits are mandated and significantly higher than in other Asian countries. Fees on transactions are determined by the Association of Banks, but banks are not permitted to change these fees without BNM approval. Credit card interest rates are capped at 18 % per annum. Presently, foreign banks are also not allowed to open Ringgit Correspondent Bank Accounts with local banks, as this is deemed as local banks being used as conduits for "branching" by foreign banks.

BNM currently allows foreign banks to open four additional branches throughout Malaysia, subject to restrictions, which include designating where the branches can be set up (i.e., in market centers, semi-urban areas and non-urban areas). The policies do not allow foreign banks to set up new branches within 1.5 km of an existing local bank. BNM has considered ATMs as equivalent to separate branches. BNM also has conditioned foreign banks' ability to offer certain services on commitments to undertake certain back office activities in Malaysia.

To attract multinational corporations (MNCs) to establish their treasury management services in Malaysia, the Malaysian government announced in its 2012 budget an income tax exemption of 70% for 5 years, a withholding tax exemption on interest payments on borrowings, and stamp duty exemption on loan and service agreements. The government has extended a concessionary tax rate of 10% on dividends of non-corporate institutional and individual investors in Real Estate Investment Trusts through December 2016. The government provides an income tax exemption of 100% for 10 years and stamp duty exemption on loan and service agreements for companies that locate in the Tun Razak Exchange, a new business center in Kuala Lumpur. In addition to the income tax exemption of 100% for 10 years and stamp duty exemption on loan and service agreements for Tun Razak Exchange (formerly known as Kuala Lumpur International Financial District) status companies, the government also in its 2013 Budget announced that these companies would enjoy industrial building allowance and accelerated capital allowance.

Insurance

The life insurance industry remains dominated by foreign providers, including some U.S. firms, while domestic firms control the general insurance industry. In 2009, foreign ownership limits were raised from 49% to 70% for branches of foreign insurance companies. However, foreign equity above 70 % is considered on a case-by-case basis for insurance companies if the investment is determined to facilitate the consolidation and rationalization of the insurance industry. Reinsurance companies are required to do more than 50% of reinsurance in Malaysia and have 5% cession and local retention. As part of Malaysia's response to the 1997-1998 Asian financial crises, all branches of foreign insurance companies were required to incorporate locally.

Investment Services

Foreigners are permitted to purchase a limited number of stockbrokerage licenses and are allowed to take a majority ownership stake in unit trust management companies. Malaysia has allowed five foreign stock brokerage firms and one foreign fund management company to set up operations in Malaysia. Maximum foreign ownership in domestic Malaysian stock brokerage firms and unit trusts is 70%. There are no foreign equity restrictions for fund management companies providing wholesale services and 70% foreign equity unit trust management companies providing retail services and for stock broking companies. Futures brokerage firms may be 100% foreign-owned. International fund managers have to go through a local fund provider, which then establishes a 'feeder' arrangement.

In 2011, Securities Commission Act 1993 and the Capital Markets and Services Act 2007 were amended to promote the development of the capital market, in line with global standards and pursuant to the strategies outlined in the Capital Market Masterplan 2. Subject to the Securities Commission's approval, fund management firms may offer a range of funds from which individuals can choose to invest in, based on their financial needs, goals and risk appetite. The Capital Market Master Plan 2 was released in April 2011. Full report: http://www.sc.com.my/eng/html/cmp2/cmp2_final.pdf

Offshore Financial Services Center

The Federal Territory of Labuan was declared an International Offshore Financial Center in October 1990. Businesses receive preferential tax treatment for offshore banking activities, trust and fund management, offshore insurance and offshore insurance-related businesses, and offshore investment holding businesses conducted in Labuan. Islamic banks and takaful (Islamic insurance) operators regulated by the Labuan Financial Services Authority are given greater flexibility to open operation offices anywhere in Malaysia and are granted a tax exemption for international currency Islamic financial businesses. Islamic banks and takaful operators retain the favored tax treatment extended to offshore businesses in Labuan, 3% or RM 20,000 (approximately US$5,650), whether or not they maintain a physical presence in Labuan. This option is not available for conventional banks, which are required to maintain a physical presence in Labuan in order to retain the favorable tax treatment.

Islamic Financial Services

The Malaysian Parliament passed legislation in late 2012 to update the regulatory framework for Islamic Financial Services. The Malaysian government provides tax incentives and other measures to encourage commercial banks operating in Malaysia to set up full-fledged Islamic banking subsidiaries. BNM uses its Malaysia International Islamic Financial Center Initiative to provide special tax and regulatory treatment, scholarships, and efforts to work toward mutual recognition of Islamic banking and takaful (Islamic insurance) practices. This offers a ten-year tax exemption on Islamic financial products in foreign currencies and tax relief for Islamic Finance studies. Expatriate Islamic finance experts are exempted from paying Malaysian income tax in an effort to better enable Malaysia to attract foreign talent. Foreign institutions can hold 70% equity ownership in domestic Islamic banks.

The Government continues to promote takaful as part of its strategy to make Malaysia a global hub for Islamic financial services, including through tax breaks and incentives. Companies wishing to offer takaful need a separate license. Foreign investors are permitted to own 49% of takaful joint ventures. International takaful operators, both domestic and foreign, may apply for licenses to conduct business in international currencies, either as incorporated entities or as branches. Currently, AIA Takaful International Berhad is the sole foreign-owned international takaful operator in Malaysia. Bank Negara is working with qualified local and foreign insurers to provide "re-takaful" (reinsurance under Islamic principles) services in Malaysia and to make Malaysia their center for re-takaful activities. New re-takaful operators will be given flexibility to conduct business in the country as a subsidiary or branch.

Malaysia has 10 international Islamic fund management firms. The government provides tax incentives for existing stock brokerage firms to set up Islamic brokerage subsidiaries and recently issued three new licenses to high profile brokerage firms, including U.S. firms Goldman Sachs and Citibank Securities, which the government hopes will attract Middle Eastern capital to invest in Malaysia. There are no restrictions on the ability of wholly foreign-owned Islamic fund management companies to invest assets abroad. Fees received from the management of Islamic funds are tax-exempt for ten years.

Maritime and Logistics

Foreigners are subject to a 70% equity limit in shipping and logistics companies and 49% in forwarding agencies. According to Malaysian officials, requirements would vary for single purpose and multipurpose port facilities.

Land and Agriculture

Only Malaysian citizens may own agricultural land. Malaysia also restricts foreign participation in agriculture (unless it is an agro-tourism linked project), and construction.

Land acquisitions by foreign interests that require approval from the Malaysian government are;

- Acquisition of agricultural land valued at US$163,000 and above
- Land of at least five acres in area for following purposes of: commercial scale agricultural activities, agro-tourism projects or agro based industrial activities for production of export goods.
- Acquisition of industrial land valued at US$163,000 and above.

The Federal Department of Land and Mines controls the incorporation of mining companies.

However, mining, land ownership and licensing requirements to mine are under the jurisdiction of each individual Malaysian State's mining departments.

There are no restrictions for investing in the fisheries industry, except for owning an aquaculture or deep sea fishing project as they are subject to the 30% local equity requirement for establishing the company. For an aquaculture project, the size of the pond must be at least two hectares in area.

Corporate Taxes

For tax purposes, local and foreign enterprises are treated essentially the same. Resident petroleum companies pay 38% income tax; all other resident companies currently pay an income tax of 25%. Dividends are taxed at the corporate rate. A company is resident in Malaysia for tax purposes if its management and control is exercised in Malaysia, that is, if directors' meetings are held in Malaysia. Payments made to non-residents for technical or management services and rental of movable properties are subject to withholding tax at the rate of 10%. Multinational corporations that establish their treasury management services in Malaysia are given 70% exemption of income taxes for 5 years, withholding taxes on interest payment on borrowings, and stamp duties on loan and services agreements. The income tax rate for non-resident individuals is 26%. The U.S. and Malaysia do not have a bilateral tax agreement and no negotiations are anticipated at this time. The government has postponed since 2010 a plan to implement a Goods and Services Tax (GST, similar to a value-added tax).

Human Resources

Beyond the investment restrictions resulting from the Bumiputra policies and often opaque regulatory process, Malaysia's shortage of skilled labor is its most oft-cited impediment to economic growth. (See sections on labor and performance requirements).

Conversion and Transfer Policies

The Malaysian central bank states that Malaysia maintains liberal foreign exchange administration policies. Selective capital controls imposed in 1998 during the Asian Financial Crisis to insulate the Malaysian economy from risks posed by volatile short-term capital flows and to eliminate offshore trading of the Malaysian Ringgit have been largely removed. A series of sequenced and progressive liberalization initiatives gradually relaxed controls on foreign direct investment flows, wages, dividends, interest, and rental income earned in Malaysia, to the point that capital now moves freely in and out of Malaysia.

The government continues to control the use of Malaysian Ringgit outside of Malaysia for settlement. However, there are no longer restrictions on resident companies with export earnings from paying in foreign currencies to another resident company for the purchase of goods and services. Foreign investors are allowed to buy or sell Malaysian Ringgit on a forward or spot basis with licensed onshore banks to facilitate the settlement of investments in Ringgit. In June 2011, Bank Negara removed limits on outbound investment, non-bank inter-company loans, and trade financing.

BNM manages a floating exchange rate against a trade-weighted basket of currencies. The exchange rate against the USD stood at 3.05 on December 31, 2012. All payments to other countries must be made through authorized foreign exchange dealers. Banks must record the amount and purpose of each cross-border transfer over RM 200,000 (approximately US$58,000). More information on Malaysia's foreign exchange administration can be found at http://www.bnm.gov.my/index.php?ch=fea_adm&pg=fea_adm&lang=en

Expropriation and Compensation

The Embassy is not aware of any cases of uncompensated expropriation of U.S.-held assets by the Malaysian government. The government's stated policy is that all investors, both foreign and domestic, are entitled to fair compensation in the event that their private property is required for public purposes. Should the investor and the government disagree on the amount of compensation, the issue is then referred to the Malaysian judicial system.

DISPUTE SETTLEMENT

Malaysia has signed and ratified the Convention on the Settlement of Investment Disputes between States and Nationals of Other States. Malaysia became a Contracting State on October 14, 1966 when the Convention entered into force, granting jurisdiction over investment disputes between the Government of Malaysia and non-Malaysian citizens to the International Center for Settlement of Investment Disputes (ICSID). https://icsid.worldbank.org/ICSID/Index.jsp Malaysia also is a signatory to the Convention on the Recognition and Enforcement of Foreign Arbitral Awards. The domestic legal system is accessible but generally requires any non-Malaysian citizen to make a large deposit before pursuing a case in the Malaysian courts (i.e., $100,000), and can be slow, bureaucratic, and is regarded by some observers as politically influenced.

Many firms choose to include mandatory arbitration clauses in their contracts. The government actively promotes use of the Kuala Lumpur Regional Center for Arbitration (http://www.rcakl.org.my), established under the auspices of the Asian-African Legal Consultative Committee to offer international arbitration, mediation, and conciliation for trade disputes. The KLRCA is the only recognized center for arbitration in Malaysia. Arbitration held in a foreign jurisdiction under the rules of the Convention on the Settlement of Investment Disputes between States and Nationals of Other States 1965 or under the United Nations Commission on International trade Law Arbitration Rules 1976 and the Rules of the Regional Centre for Arbitration at Kuala Lumpur can be enforceable in Malaysia.

PERFORMANCE REQUIREMENTS AND INCENTIVES

Fiscal incentives granted to both foreign and domestic investors historically have been subject to performance requirements, usually in the form of export targets, local content requirements and technology transfer requirements. Performance requirements are usually written into the individual manufacturing licenses of local and foreign investors.

The Malaysian government extends a full tax exemption incentive of fifteen years for firms with "Pioneer Status" (companies promoting products or activities in industries or parts of Malaysia to which the government places a high priority), and ten years for companies with "Investment Tax Allowance" status (those on which the government places a priority, but not as high as Pioneer Status). However, the government appears to have some flexibility with respect to the expiry of these periods, and some firms reportedly have had their pioneer status renewed. Government priorities generally include the levels of value-added, technology used, and industrial linkages. If a firm (foreign or domestic) fails to meet the terms of its license, it risks losing any tax benefits it may have been awarded. Potentially, a firm could lose its manufacturing license. The New Economic Model stated that in the long term, the government intends gradually to eliminate most of the fiscal incentives now offered to foreign and domestic manufacturing investors. More information on specific incentives for various sectors can be found at www.mida.gov.my.

Malaysia also seeks to attract foreign investment in the information technology industry, particularly in the Multimedia Super Corridor (MSC), a government scheme to foster the growth of research, development, and other high technology activities in Malaysia. Foreign investors who obtain MSC status receive tax and regulatory exemptions as well as public service commitments in exchange for a commitment of substantial technology transfer. For further details on incentives, see www.mdec.my. The Multimedia Development Corporation (MDeC) approves all applications for MSC status.

In the services sector, the government's stated goal is to attract foreign investment in regional distribution centers, international procurement centers, operational headquarter research and development, university and graduate education, integrated market and logistics support services, cold chain facilities, central utility facilities, industrial training, and environmental management. To date, Malaysia has had some success in attracting regional distribution centers and local campuses of foreign universities. For example, during 2011 the government facilitated partnerships between local partners and MIT to develop a graduate program in logistics management and with Johns Hopkins University to develop its first graduate medical school located outside the United States.

Malaysia seeks to attract foreign investment in biotechnology, but sends a mixed message on agricultural and food biotechnology. On July 8, 2010, the Malaysian Ministry of Health posted amendments to the Food Regulations 1985 [P.U. (A) 437/1985] that require strict mandatory labeling of food and food ingredients obtained through modern biotechnology. The amendments also included a requirement that no person shall import, prepare or advertise for sale, or sell any food or food ingredients obtained through modern biotechnology without the prior written approval of the Director. There is no 'threshold' level on the labeling requirement. Labeling of "GMO Free" or "Non-GMO" is not permitted. The labeling requirements only apply to foods and food ingredients obtained through modern biotechnology but not to food produced with GMO feed. The labeling regulation was originally scheduled to be enforced beginning in July 2012. However, a Ministry of Health circular published on August 27, 2012 announced that enforcement would be deferred until July 8, 2014. A copy of the law and regulations respectively can be found at: http://www.biosafety.nre.gov.my/BiosafetyAct2007.shtml, and http://www.biosafety.nre.gov.my/BIOSAFETY%20REGULATIONS%202010.pdf.

RIGHT TO PRIVATE OWNERSHIP AND ESTABLISHMENT

Foreigners may purchase property worth over RM500, 000 (approximately US$163,000) without restriction. Although the Federal government no longer requires foreigners to get approval from the FICs (Foreign Investment Committee) for the purchase of residential property, the State governments at times can be more restrictive than Federal regulation and can delay the purchase.

Owning a business in Malaysia requires two local directors, though 100% of the shares can be held by foreign owners, except in sectors where foreign investment is restricted.

PROTECTION OF PROPERTY RIGHTS

Real Property Rights

Land administration is shared among federal, state, and local government. State governments have their own rules about land ownership, including foreign ownership. Malaysian law affords strong protections to real property owners. Real property titles are recorded in public records and attorneys review transfer documentation to ensure efficacy of a title transfer. There is no title insurance available in Malaysia. Malaysian courts protect property ownership rights. Foreign investors are allowed to borrow using real property as collateral. Foreign and domestic lenders are able to record mortgages with competent authorities and execute foreclosure in the event of loan default.

Intellectual Property Rights

Malaysia was removed from the U.S. Special 301 Watch List in 2012 following improvements in recent years in protecting IPR. In December 2011, the Malaysian Parliament passed amendments to the copyright law designed to, inter alia, bring the country into compliance with the WIPO Copyright Treaty and the WIPO Performance and Phonogram Treaty, define Internet Service Provider (ISP) liabilities, and prohibit unauthorized camcording of motion pictures in theaters. Malaysia subsequently acceded to the WIPO Copyright Treaty and the WIPO Performance and Phonogram Treaty in September 2012. In addition, the Ministry of Domestic Trade, Cooperatives, and Consumerism (MDTCC) took steps to enhance Malaysia's enforcement regime, including active cooperation with rights holders on matters pertaining to IPR enforcement, ongoing training of prosecutors for specialized IPR courts, and the reestablishment of a Special Anti-Piracy Taskforce. In recent years, the MDTCC has also instructed its enforcement division to begin to take *ex officio* action, resulting in significant seizures of pirated products. In June 2011, the Malaysian government took action to block access to several international pirate sites and continues to be open to take down local sites featuring pirated content. The Ministry of Health implemented regulations in 2011 to provide a five year term for data protection of pharmaceutical products.

Despite Malaysia's success in improving its effective protection of IPR, key issues remain, including relatively widespread availability of pirated and counterfeit products in Malaysia, high rates of piracy over the Internet, and continued problems with book piracy. The United States continues to encourage Malaysia to accede to the WIPO Budapest Treaty on the International Recognition of the Deposit of Microorganisms for the Purposes of Patent Procedure. In addition, the United States continues to urge Malaysia to provide effective protection against unfair commercial use, as well as unauthorized disclosure, of undisclosed test or other data generated to obtain marketing approval for pharmaceutical products, and to provide an effective system to address patent issues expeditiously in connection with applications to market pharmaceutical products.

Copyright Protection and Optical Media Piracy

Copyright protection lasts for 50 years after the author's death and extends to computer software. The Copyright Act includes enforcement provisions allowing government officials to enter and search premises suspected of infringement and to seize infringing copies and reproduction equipment. The amendments to the Act passed by the Malaysian Parliament in 2011 include new authority to combat camcording activities in cinemas.

Malaysia continues to face challenges in ensuring the effective protection of copyrighted materials. Pirated optical discs remain widely available, although less conspicuously than in the past. Unauthorized photocopying of textbooks remains a particular concern. On-line piracy and illegal downloading of cinematographic and musical works has grown.

The Optical Disc Act of 2000 established a licensing and regulatory framework to control the manufacture of optical discs and to fight piracy. Under the Act, manufacturers are required to obtain licenses from MITI and MDTCC, to place source identification (SID) codes on each disc, and to allow regular inspections of their operations.

Pharmaceuticals

The Ministry of Health in 2011 issued revised regulations to provide data exclusivity protection for pharmaceuticals for five years for new chemical entities, and three years for new indications. The time periods would be based on a drug's approval date in its country of origin. Applications for data exclusivity for new chemical entities must be made within 18 months from the date the product is first registered and granted marketing authorization and for second indications within 12 months from the date the second indication is approved. The Malaysian law allows for the regulatory approval of generic versions of pharmaceuticals that are still patented, but prohibits marketing and commercial manufacturing during the patent validity period.

Sales of counterfeit pharmaceuticals remain a problem in Malaysia. Counterfeit medicines that have been identified include "drugs" with the wrong ingredients, insufficient active ingredients, and those with fake packaging. Unregistered generic copies of patented products are also available in Malaysia. The Ministry of Health and the MDTCC are improving their enforcement efforts, and share information and collaborate with industry on those efforts. The Ministry of Health in late 2012 circulated for comment draft legislation that would, if passed by Parliament, significantly increase penalties against those selling counterfeit medicines.

Trademarked Consumer Products

A number of U.S. consumer product companies also have suffered losses due to the presence in the market of counterfeit trademarked products. Counterfeiters have improved the quality of packaging and marketing so that consumers are misled into purchasing the products. Most of these counterfeit products are brought into the country from China, Thailand, and India.

In 2011, MDTCC launched a "Basket of Brands" initiative, a voluntary program where participating trademark holders receive more proactive protection efforts in exchange for a commitment to testify in any resulting prosecutions. Complicating enforcement of trademark-related violations is a Malaysian Court of Appeals interpretation of the trademark law that requires enforcement officials to have a "Trade Description Order" to conduct criminal raids when the counterfeit product seized is not identical to the trademarked original.

Patents

Patents registered in Malaysia generally have 20-year duration from date of filing, which can be extended under certain circumstances. The length of time required for patent registration averages five years and trademark registration averages two years. Registrations are handled by the MDTCC's Patents and Trademarks Department.

Transparency of Regulatory System

The lack of transparency in government rule-making and procedures in Malaysia has impeded U.S. firms' access to the Malaysian market. Stakeholders have found it very difficult to access draft laws and regulations for the purpose of reviewing and offering comments, in large part due to Malaysia's broad Official Secrets Act.

Following an announcement by Prime Minister Najib in February 2012, the Chief Secretary to the Cabinet in April 2012 issued a circular instructing all Ministries to publicly post all draft laws and regulations on the internet for a 14 day public comment period. However, implementation of this new requirement appears to be uneven and many Ministries continue to consult selected stake holders in an opaque invitation-only manner.

Government Procurement

Malaysia is an observer but not a signatory of the WTO Government Procurement Agreement (GPA). Malaysia's procurement policies are explicitly used to encourage greater participation of Bumiputra in the economy, transfer technology to local industries, create opportunities for local companies in the services sector, and enhance Malaysia's export capabilities.

U.S. companies have voiced concerns about the non-transparent nature of the procurement process in Malaysia. Traditionally, international tenders have been invited only where domestic goods and services are not available. In domestic tenders, preferences are provided for Bumiputra suppliers and other domestic suppliers. As a result, foreign companies do not have the same opportunities as local companies to compete for contracts. In most government tenders, especially for major infrastructure, foreign companies are required to take on a Bumiputra partner before their bids will be considered.

Government officials maintain that procurement reform is an important goal of the Najib administration, and that progress is being made. The Prime Minister established the Performance Management and Delivery Unit (PEMANDU), to address concerns about transparency and competitive bidding in government procurement. In April 2010, the government launched a website to improve transparency in public procurement. Known as the MyProcurement portal, which can be accessed at http://myprocurement.treasury.gov.my, the website aims to be a government procurement information centre. To date, more than 5,000 contracts are listed on the website citing information on both advertised and awarded tenders (including dates), values of the contracts, and winners of the tenders. Malaysia is also increasing use of the Swiss Challenge method and integrity pacts in its government procurement procedures. However, some of the largest infrastructure and other projects are still sole-sourced through closed negotiations, not open tenders.

CORRUPTION

Malaysia ranked in 54th place in Transparency International's Corruption Perception Index in 2012 (the lower the ranking, the less perceived corruption). The Malaysian government has taken steps to address corruption, including through the establishment of the Malaysian Anti-Corruption Commission (MACC) in 2008, passage of legislation to make judicial appointments more transparent (the Judicial Appointments Commission Act) also in 2008, passage of a Whistleblower Protection Act in 2010, the introduction of procurement reforms and the launch of government initiatives to target corrupt practices. The Malaysian government considers bribery a criminal act and does not permit bribes to be deducted from taxes. Malaysia's anti-corruption law includes the criminal offense of bribery of foreign public officials, permits the prosecution of Malaysians for offense committed overseas, and also provides for the seizure of properties.

Critics have questioned the MACC's ability to effectively address high-level corruption, although a number of cases are in court. The MACC conducts investigations but prosecutorial discretion remains with the Attorney General. A lack of capacity and technical skills in some areas hampers MACC's overall effectiveness. The MACC introduced a public database of those convicted of corruption offenses. There is no systematic public disclosure of assets by senior officials. Critics also note that the Whistleblower Act does not protect those who disclose allegations to the media.

Government officials cite a four point approach to reducing corruption in government procurement, a key area of focus: increasing the number and decreasing the size of government procurement contract subject to open tenders, introducing the Transparency International "Integrity Pact" concept to be signed by all vendors that they understand bidding rules and anti-corruption laws prior to engaging in contract negotiations, issuing rules against Ministerial "referral letters" recommending specific contractors for government contracts, and fully implementing the new Whistleblower Act.

Efficient Capital Markets and Portfolio Investments

Banking

Foreign investors and foreign companies have access to credit on the local capital market. Foreign-controlled companies may seek any amount of Malaysian Ringgit credit facilities without Bank Negara's approval. There are no restrictions on foreign stock brokerage companies obtaining ringgit facilities to facilitate the settlement of transaction on the Malaysian stock and bond markets. There is no limit on the number of residential and commercial property loans allowed to foreigners. In 2008, the government liberalized the foreign exchange administration rules allowing borrowing in foreign currency by residents as well as borrowing and lending in ringgit between residents and non-residents.

The Malaysian Deposit Insurance Company insures deposit accounts of up to RM 250,000 (US$80,645) with separate funds for conventional and Islamic banking institutions.

Capital Markets and Securities Trading

Foreigners may trade in securities and derivatives. Malaysia houses Asia's third largest corporate bond market, behind only Japan and Korea in market capitalization. Both domestic and foreign companies regularly access capital in Malaysia's bond market. Malaysia provides tax incentives for foreign companies issuing Islamic bonds and financial instruments in Malaysia. During 2011, foreign capital continued flowing back into Malaysian bonds after a US$35 billion outflow during the 2008-9 global financial crises.

Malaysia's stock market (Bursa Malaysia) is open to foreign investment and foreign corporation issuing shares. However, foreign issuers remain subject to Bumiputra ownership requirements of 12.5% if the majority of their operations are in Malaysia. Listing requirements for foreign companies are similar to that of local companies. There additional criteria for foreign companies wanting to list in Malaysia including, among others: approval of regulatory authorities of foreign jurisdiction where the company was incorporated, valuation of assets that are standards applied in Malaysia or

International Valuation Standards and the company must have been registered with the Registrar of Companies under the Companies Act 1965.

Malaysia has taken steps to promote good corporate governance by listed companies. Publicly listed companies must submit quarterly reports that include a balance sheet and income statement within two months of each financial quarter's end and audited annual accounts for public scrutiny within four months of each year's end. An individual may hold up to 25 corporate directorships. All public and private company directors are required to attend classes on corporate rules and regulations.

Legislation also regulates equity buybacks, mandates book entry of all securities transfers, and requires that all owners of securities accounts be identified. A Central Depository System (CDS) for stocks and bonds established in 1991 makes physical possession of certificates unnecessary. All shares traded on the Bursa Malaysia must be deposited in the CDS. Short selling of stocks is prohibited.

Competition and State-Owned Enterprises

On April 21, 2010, the Parliament of Malaysia approved two bills, the Competition Commission Act 2010 and the Competition Act 2010. The Acts took effect January 1, 2012. The Competition Act prohibits cartels and abuses of a dominant market position, but does not create any pre-transaction review of mergers or acquisitions. Violations are punishable by fines, as well as imprisonment for individual violations. The Acts established a Competition Commission with broad investigative and enforcement powers, as well as a Competition Appeals Tribunal (CAT) to hear all appeals of Commission decisions.

State-owned enterprises play a very significant role in the Malaysian economy. Such enterprises have been used to spearhead infrastructure and industrial projects. The government owns approximately 36% of the value of firms listed on the Bursa Malaysia through its seven Government-Linked Investment Corporations (GLICs), including a majority stake in a number of companies. Only a minority portion of stock is available for trading for some of the largest publicly listed local companies. The government has indicated increasing interest in restarting its privatization efforts through the New Economic Model reforms. Khazanah, often considered the government's sovereign wealth fund, owns stakes in companies competing many of the country's major industries. The Prime Minister chairs Khazanah's Board of Directors. PETRONAS, the state-owned oil and gas company, is Malaysia's only Fortune Global 500 firm.

In July 2011, the Government identified 33 government-linked companies as ready for divestment, but did not identify them by name. Under the plan to rationalize the portfolio of government-linked companies (GLCs) in Malaysia, the Government will reduce its stakes in some of these companies, list a few others and sell the rest. In first quarter of 2012 Khazanah offloaded its stake in the national car company Proton to DRB-Hicom Bhd. In December 2012 Khazanah announced its intention to divest its IT company Time Engineering Bhd to a Bumiputra-owned company. However, the majority of GLCs are not affected by the divestment plan, and GLCs will retain a major role in Malaysia's economy.

Corporate Social Responsibility (CSR)

The development of corporate social responsibility in Malaysia is moving to higher levels and many larger companies have CSR programs and activities. In 2006, Malaysian stock market regulator, the Securities Commission, published a CSR Framework for all publicly listed companies, which are required to disclose their CSR programs in their annual financial reports.

In 2007 the Women, Family and Community Ministry launched the Prime Minister's CSR's Awards to recognize companies that have made a difference to the communities in which they are active through their CSR programs.

Political Violence

Malaysia has experienced political stability since its independence in 1957, with the exception of ethnic riots that followed the 1969 national elections. Najib Razak peacefully took office as Malaysia's 6th Prime Minister on April 2, 2009. The government historically denied assembly permits for anti-government street demonstrations. In April 2012, the Peaceful Assembly Act took effect, which eliminates the need for permits for public assemblies but outlaws street protests and places other significant restrictions on public assemblies. On April 28 2012, the police disrupted a large protest march that took place despite restrictions the government attempted to impose. Subsequent demonstrations and protest marches took place in 2012 without disruption.

Bilateral Investment and Taxation Agreements

Malaysia has bilateral investment guarantee agreements with over 70 economies, including the United States, has bilateral investment treaties with 36 countries, and has double taxation treaties with over 70 countries. Malaysia's double taxation agreement with the U.S. currently is limited to air and sea transportation. There is currently no bilateral investment treaty between the US and Malaysia.

OPIC and Other Investment Insurance Programs

Malaysia has a limited investment guarantee agreement with the U.S. under the U.S. Overseas Private Investment Corporation (OPIC) program, for which it has qualified since 1959. However, few investors have sought OPIC insurance in Malaysia.

Labor

Malaysia's shortage of skilled labor is the most often cited impediment to economic growth cited in numerous studies. Malaysia has an acute shortage of highly qualified professionals, scientists, and academics.

The Malaysian labor market operates at essentially full employment, with unemployment for Malaysians averaging 3.2% in 2012. The number of unemployed university graduates remains high, however, at about 40,000 in 2012. In an effort to improve the employability of local graduates, the GOM offers additional training modules at public universities in English language skills, presentation techniques, and entrepreneurship.

Malaysia is a member of the International Labor Organization (ILO). Labor relations in Malaysia are generally non-confrontational. A system of government controls strongly discourages strikes. Some labor disputes are settled through negotiation or arbitration by an industrial court, though cases can be backlogged for years. Once a case is referred to the industrial court, the union and management are barred from further industrial action.

While national unions are proscribed due to sovereignty issues within Malaysia, there are a number of territorial federations of unions (the three territories being Peninsular Malaysia, Sabah, and Sarawak). The government has prevented some trade unions, such as those in the electronics and textile sectors, from forming territorial federations. Instead of allowing a federation for all of Peninsular Malaysia, the electronics sector is limited to forming four regional federations of unions, while the textile sector is limited to state-based federations of unions, for those states which have a textile industry. Employers and employees share the costs of the *Social Security Organization* (SOSCO), which covers an estimated 12.9 million workers. No systematic welfare programs or government unemployment benefits exist; however the Employee Provident Fund (EPF), which employers and employees are required to contribute to, provides retirement benefits for workers in the private sector. Civil servants receive pensions upon retirement.

The regulation of employment in Malaysia, specifically as it affects the hiring and redundancy of workers remains a notable impediment to employing workers in Malaysia. The high cost of terminating their employees, even in cases of wrongdoing, is a source of complaint for domestic and foreign employers. The World Bank estimates that the financial cost of firing an employee averages 75 weeks of salary for that worker.

The Embassy hears reports from some U.S. companies that the government monitors the ethnic balance among employees and enforces an ethnic quota system for hiring in certain areas. Race-based preferences in hiring and promotion are widespread in government, government-owned universities, and government-linked corporations.

The Minimum Wage Order 2012 came into force on January 1, 2013 and fixed the rate at $300 per month in Peninsular Malaysia and $266 for those in East Malaysia. However there have been calls for the government to defer the implementation of the new policy.

Employing Expatriates

Foreign workers are categorized as follows: "expatriates" (anyone earning at least RM 5,000 or $1,429, per month); "foreign skilled workers," and "foreign unskilled and semi-skilled workers." The Malaysian Government has embarked on a number of immigration liberalization initiatives aimed at expatriates and foreign skilled workers.

Employing expatriates involves two phases. First, the company must be granted approval for the expatriate post; then the individual must be approved by receiving a "reference visa" from the Malaysian embassy in the expatriate's home country and approval from the Immigration Department. More details can be found at www.pemudah.gov.my/guidebook.pdf.

Companies in different sectors must apply for approval for expatriate posts through the respective government authority: manufacturing and manufacturing-related companies apply through MIDA; companies with "Multimedia Super Corridor" (MSC) status through the Multimedia Development Corporation; banking and insurance companies through Bank Negara Malaysia; securities brokers through the Securities Commission; biotechnology companies through Biotech Corp; and companies in other sectors through the Expatriate Committee. Each authority has its own set of requirements and decisions are made on a case-by-case basis.

Manufacturing companies that are 100% foreign-owned must have a minimum paid-in capital of RM 500,000 (as of January 1, 2010) to employ expatriates. Companies with joint foreign and Malaysian ownership must have a minimum paid-up capital of RM 350,000 while Malaysian-owned companies must have a minimum of RM 250,000. It appears that the larger a company's paid-in capital, the more expatriates the company can employ. Manufacturing-related companies in sub-sectors targeted by the government for development are given priority. These include regional establishments (operational headquarters, international procurement centers, regional distribution centers); support services (integrated logistics services, integrated market support services, central utility facilities, cold chain facilities); research and development; software development; hotel and tourism projects; technical and vocational training; some environment-related services; and film or video production. Except for manufacturing companies with automatic allowances, a firm wishing to employ expatriate personnel generally must demonstrate that there is a shortage of qualified Malaysian candidates and that a Malaysian citizen is being trained. In practice this is difficult for firms to document. In 2010, the government eliminated the six-month waiting period for determining a shortage of Malaysian candidates.

Expatriate visas are issued for a period of up to ten years. Unskilled foreign workers receive a three-year work permit, renewable annually up to five years, and foreign skilled workers can qualify for up to 12 months. If an unskilled worker acquires "skills certificates," he/she may apply for a permit as a skilled worker after exhausting the five-year maximum as an unskilled worker. Foreign domestic helpers are permitted to remain in Malaysia on a work permit beyond ten years. Malaysia's freeze on permanent resident visas was removed in 2010 with a point system introduced for residents living in Malaysia over five years. Malaysia also has the "Malaysia, My Second Home" program and the Residence Pass that provides long-term resident visas for expatriates. Launched in April 2011, the Residence Pass – Talent (RP-T) is offered to highly qualified expatriates who can contribute towards Malaysia's economic transformation. The ten-year Pass accords eligible holders many benefits, including the ability to change employers without having to renew the pass. Details are at http://www.talentcorp.com.my.

Government officials say they have taken steps to simplify and expedite permit approvals for some categories of foreign personnel. The PEMUDAH task force developed a guidebook clarifying the various procedures and requirements. In 2010, the government implemented new regulations reducing application approval times, removing expatriate age limits, and allowing automatic approval for expatriate employees earning over US$2,580 per month. The spouse of an expatriate holding a Dependent Pass is allowed to take up paid employment without converting the Dependent Pass to an "Employment Pass" or to a "Visit Pass for Temporary Employment" on the condition that permission to take up the paid employment is endorsed on his/her passport by an authorized Immigration officer.

In November 2012, the government announced the setting up of the Expatriate Services Division to facilitate and retain foreign talents. Expected to be fully operational by March 2013, this division will be an integrated service facility offering services to expatriates and their dependants in matters relating to immigration process.

FOREIGN TRADE ZONES/FREE PORTS

The Free Zone Act of 1990 authorized the Minister of Finance to designate any suitable area as either a Free Industrial Zone (FIZ), where manufacturing and assembly takes place, or a Free Commercial Zone (FCZ), generally for warehousing commercial stock. Currently there are 13 FIZs and 12 FCZs in Malaysia. In June 2006, the Port Klang Free Zone opened as the nation's first fully integrated FIZ and FCZ, although the project been dogged by corruption allegations related to the land acquisition for the site. The

Minister of Finance may appoint any federal, state, or local government agency or entity as an authority to administer, maintain and operate any free trade zone.

Raw materials, products and equipment may be imported duty-free into these zones with minimum customs formalities. Companies that export not less than 80% of their output and depend on imported goods, raw materials, and components may be located in these FZs. Ports, shipping and maritime-related services play an important role in Malaysia since 90% of its international trade by volume is seaborne. Malaysia is also a major transshipment center.

Goods sold into the Malaysian economy by companies within the FZs must pay import duties. If a company wants to enjoy Common External Preferential Tariff (CEPT) rates within the ASEAN Free Trade Area, 40% of a product's content must be ASEAN-sourced. In addition to the FZs, Malaysia permits the establishment of licensed manufacturing warehouses outside of free zones, which give companies greater freedom of location while allowing them to enjoy privileges similar to firms operating in an FZ. Companies operating in these zones require approval/license for each activity. The time needed to obtain licenses depends on the type of approval and ranges from 2-8 weeks.

FOREIGN DIRECT INVESTMENT STATISTICS

The U.S. has been consistently a leading foreign investor in Malaysia, with significant presence in the oil and gas sector, manufacturing, and financial services. A 2005 survey by the American Malaysian Chamber of Commerce put cumulative U.S. interest in Malaysia at more than US $30.0 billion, significantly more than some official U.S. and Malaysian statistics, which may not capture or may undercount U.S. investment. U.S. firms with significant investment in Malaysia's petroleum and petrochemical sector include: ExxonMobil, Caltex, ConocoPhillips, Murphy Oil, Hess Oil, Halliburton, Dow Chemical and Eastman Chemicals. Major semiconductor manufacturers, including Freescale, Texas Instruments, Intel, and others have substantial operations in Malaysia, as do electronics manufacturers Western Digital, Komag, Agilent, and Motorola. In recent years Malaysia has attracted significant investment in the production of solar panels, including from U.S. firms. Virtually all major Japanese consumer electronics firms (Sony, Fuji, Panasonic, Matsushita, Hitachi, etc.) have facilities in Malaysia. Tables 1-3 report approved manufacturing investment in Malaysia, as opposed to actual investments, and do not include significant U.S. investment in the petroleum and financial sectors.

Table 1. Sources of Approved Manufacturing Investment in Malaysia
(Value in Millions of U.S. Dollars)

	2006	2007	2008	2009	2010	2011	Jan- Sept 2012
Total Investment	**12,532**	**17,422**	**18,146**	**9,543**	**15,317**	**17,693**	**10,399**
Foreign	5,512	9,717	13,323	6,475	9,434	10,772	5,145
Domestic	7,021	7,705	4,823	3,068	5,883	6,920	5,254

Source: Malaysian Investment Development Authority.
Exchange Rates: U.S. $1.0=RM 3.42 (2009 rate), RM3.04 (2010 rate), 3.17 (2011 rate)
Note: Approved manufacturing investment only, does not include the upstream oil and gas industry or services. "Approved investments" represent planned or proposed investment, not actual investment flows.

Table 2. Leading Approved Foreign Investment Sources in the Manufacturing Sector
(Value in Millions of U.S. Dollars; Share in %)

	2006	2007	2008	2009	2010	2011	Jan-Sept 2012
Germany	63	1,092	1,287	124	629	650	94
United States	675	878	2,544	672	3,811	836	60
Singapore	514	858	565	585	700	825	550
Netherlands	895	491	526	140	303	336	255
Japan	1,202	1,896	1,637	2,047	1,308	3,367	754
Australia	698	490	3,830	94	N/A	97	13
Hong Kong	N/A	N/A	24	1,550	898	131	6
China	N/A	N/A	10	47	N/A	398	84
Korea	N/A	N/A	58	98	N/A	1,728	202
Total Foreign	5,512	9,717	13,323	6,475	9,434	11,382	5,254
U.S. Share of Total Foreign	12.2%	9.0%	19.1%	10.4%	49.8%	7.3%	1.1%
Foreign Share of Total	44.0%	55.8%	73.4%	67.9%	81.0%	60.4%	50.5%

Source: Malaysian Investment Development Authority.
Exchange Rates: U.S. $1.0=RM 3.42 (2009 rate), RM3.04 (2010 rate), 3.17 (2011 rate)
Note: Approved manufacturing investment only, does not include the upstream oil and gas industry or services. "Approved investments" represent planned or proposed investment, not actual investment flows.

Table 3. Approved Foreign Manufacturing Investment by Sector
(Value in Millions of U.S. Dollars)

Sector	2006	2007	2008	2009	2010	2011	Jan-Sept 2012
Chemicals	826	454	357	2,058	564	1,015	2,167
Petroleum Products	165	1,551	364	135	354	N/A	N/A
Electronics	2,344	3,993	5,068	1,162	3,844	5,900	557
Basic Metal	623	1,450	5,978	127	1,167	1,131	446
Food Manufacturing	244	107	313	273	N/A	810	248
Transport	59	89	249	158	N/A	336	379
Other	685	2,073	994	2,562	N/A	N/A	N/A
Total	5,512	9,717	13,323	6,475	5,929	9,192	3,797

Source: Malaysian Investment Development Authority.

Exchange Rates: U.S. $1.0=RM 3.42 (2009 rate), RM3.04 (2010 rate), 3.17 (2011 rate)

Note: Approved manufacturing investment only, does not include the upstream oil and gas industry or services. "Approved investments" represent planned or proposed investment, not actual investment flows.

Table 4. Foreign Direct Investment Flow in Malaysia by Countries
(Value in Millions of U.S Dollars)

	2008	2009	2010	2011	2012		
					1Q	2Q	3Q
Singapore	4,723	4,093	3,814	5,748	1,042	1,461	1,459
United States	3,823	1,277	5,382	3,966	346	1,266	1,585
Japan	2,637	2,519	3,311	5,584	1,091	749	1,002
Netherlands	2,637	2,134	4,066	2,784	572	492	949
Hong Kong, SAR	1,867	2,357	1,278	2,377	755	854	744
Germany	1,342	1,009	1,303	2,112	346	212	349
Thailand	1,180	889	841	854	128	149	181
Korea, Republic of	295	377	1,726	364	82	261	92
Cayman Islands	1,650	47	112	466	340	67	176
Australia	418	436	409	500	200	212	446
Bermuda	586	424	173	506	130	204	48
Virgin Islands (British)	517	554	592	-67	-37	224	200
China	372	264	343	313	165	90	84
Chinese Taipei	551	147	142	343	149	101	47

Source: Bank Negara Malaysia and Department of Statistics Malaysia.

Exchange Rates: U.S. $1.0=RM 3.42 (2009 rate), RM3.04 (2010 rate), RM3.17 (2011 rate) RM3.05 (2012 rate).

Note: Credit refers to inflow of funds or amounts received by direct investment enterprise in Malaysia from foreign direct investor and affiliate in the form of equity capital, reinvested earnings, loan transactions, and trade credits as well as other capital receipts.

Table 5. Foreign Direct Investment Stock, Countries
(Value in Millions of U.S Dollars)

	2008	2009	2010	2011
Singapore	15,095.80	15,956.20	17,549.20	22,146.00
Japan	10,504.20	10,803.90	12,499.20	15,662.60
United States	12,050.90	10,375.60	11,431.90	12,799.90
Netherlands	7,875.70	8,376.90	9,169.20	9,956.90
Chinese Taipei	724.1	733.6	644.3	615.2
Virgin Islands (British)	4,579.60	5,022.10	5,525.60	5,516.80
Germany	4,063.70	4,136.90	4,177.10	5,151.00
Hong Kong, SAR	2,100.60	2,969.60	3,905.20	3,818.30
Australia	793.20	1,966.70	2,969.70	3,419.70
Korea, Republic of	909.40	1,060.40	2,648.70	2,793.70
Cayman Islands	2,449.90	2,425.40	2,838.80	1,055.40
Bermuda	1,697.80	1,819.60	2,203.40	2,875.80
China	363.40	228.20	335.10	375.40
Thailand	227.9	86.2	-175.3	84.00

Source: Bank Negara Malaysia and Department of Statistics, Malaysia.
Exchange Rates: U.S. $1.0=RM 3.42 (2009 rate), RM3.04 (2010 rate), RM3.17 (2011 rate) RM3.05 (2012 rate).

Table 6. Foreign Direct Investment Stock in Malaysia, by Sector
(Value in Millions of U.S. Dollars)

	2008	2009	2010	2011
Manufacturing	41,756.00	42,225.70	48,918.60	57,396.20
Financial and Insurance/Takaful Activities	17,861.60	21,429.20	24,632.00	27,118.20
Information and Communication	6,567.00	5,754.70	7,149.90	8,464.90
Wholesale and Retail Trade	6,268.20	7,089.90	8,503.20	10,106.00
Mining and Quarrying (including oil and gas)	4,889.90	5,718.50	6,121.70	7,864.90
Agriculture, Forestry and Fishing	2,930.10	3,070.40	3,119.80	3,157.10
Construction	372.1	350.6	456.8	461.7
Other Services	4,340.00	4,533.00	5,433.30	6,544.20
Total	84,984.90	90,172.00	104,335.30	121,113.20

Source: Bank Negara Malaysia and Department of Statistics, Malaysia
Exchange Rates: U.S. $1.0=RM 3.42 (2009 rate), RM3.04 (2010 rate), RM3.17 (2011 rate) RM3.05 (2012 rate)
Note: Includes investments by holding companies.

WEB RESOURCES

- Bank Negara Malaysia: www.bnm.gov.my
- Securities Commission: www.sc.com.my
- MIDA: http://www.mida.gov.my
- World Intellectual Property Organization (WIPO): www.wipo.int/
- LawNet : www.lawnet.com.my
- E-Warta: http://www.e-warta.com.my/
- MITI: http://www.miti.gov.my/
- Companies Commission: http://www.ssm.com.my/
- MyIPO: http://www.myipo.gov.my/

U.S. exporters seeking general export information/assistance or country-specific commercial information should consult with their nearest Export Assistance Center or the U.S. Department of Commerce's Trade Information Center at (800) USA-TRADE, or go to the following website: http://www.export.gov. To the best of our knowledge, the information contained in this report is accurate as of the date published. However, The Department of State does not take responsibility for actions readers may take based on the information contained herein. Readers should always conduct their own due diligence before entering into business ventures or other commercial arrangements. The Department of Commerce can assist companies in these endeavors.

INDEX

A

D

E

F

G

H

I

J

K

L

M

N

O

P

Q

R

S

T

U

V

W

Y